75p

pr...

r

AFRICA'S
CHILDREN

Save the Children

Headway · Hodder & Stoughton

The Save the Children Fund would like to thank The Wiggins Teape Group Limited for donating the paper for this book.

ISBN 0 340 52709 9

First published 1990
© The Save the Children Fund 1990

The Save the Children Fund
Mary Datchelor House
17 Grove Lane
London SE5 8RD

Typeset by Wearside Tradespools, Fulwell, Sunderland
Printed in Great Britain for the educational publishing division of
Hodder and Stoughton Ltd, Mill Road, Dunton Green, Sevenoaks, Kent
by M. & A. Thomson Litho Ltd, East Kilbride

Contents

International Save the Children Alliance (ISCA

The Save the Children Fund is a member of the International Save the Children Alliance. The Alliance, with its office in Geneva, comprises the following 21 independent Save the Children organisations:

SCF-Australia; Rettet das Kind–Austria; SCF-Canada; Red Barnet–Denmark; FUDECO–Dominican Republic; SCF–Egypt; Barnabati–The Faroe Islands; Alianza para Desarrollo Juvenil Communitario–Guatemala; Soste ta Pedia–Greece; SCF–Japan; KOSAVE–Korea; SCF–Lesotho; SCF–Malawi; SCF–Mauritius; FUNDECAI–Mexico; Stichting Redt de Kinderen–The Netherlands; SCF–New Zealand; Redd Barna–Norway; Radda Barnen–Sweden; SCF–United Kingdom; Save the Children Federation–USA.

International Save the Children Alliance, 147 rue de Lausanne, CH-1202 Geneva, Switzerland.

Foreword by HRH The Princess Royal

It is nearly sixty years since the Save the Children Fund helped to organise the first International Conference on African Children, held in Geneva in June 1931. It was an effective means of extending to African children the first Declaration of the Rights of the Child, adopted by the League of Nations a few years earlier.

With the recent publication of the UN Convention on the Rights of the Child, this is an appropriate time for Save the Children to publish a new report on the prospects for Africa's children, based on its experience in many parts of Africa.

Africa has made huge strides forward in terms of its health and education and of the achievements of its people. Yet new problems have arisen to confront new generations of children. During the last decade and more, because of the multiple strains caused by war, poverty, world recession and debt, many African countries have had to endure especially severe economic hardship.

While African countries are coping with these problems, it is important that those who wish to help understand all the complexities involved. Without up-to-date knowledge and awareness, our concern is wasted and our response misdirected. Voluntary organisations like Save the Children are in daily contact with children in need. They see the suffering at first hand and are well placed to describe the causes and because of that knowledge, to attempt to evaluate and contribute to the solutions which are being offered.

I warmly recommend anyone who would like to help children or to understand Africa better to read these stories. In many cases they are told by the children themselves. Some are chilling; others are encouraging. All of them are true, written from personal experience and often requiring considerable personal effort. If we can all learn from those experiences, then their efforts will not have been in vain.

Anne

President, The Save the Children Fund
Chairman of the Africa Review Group

Acknowledgements

Prospects for Africa's Children was edited by John Montagu for the Save the Children Fund, supported by the staff of SCF's Education Unit under the direction of Andrew Hutchinson.

The editorial team would like to thank all the staff of SCF in Africa and the UK and other organisations and individuals named in this book who have contributed articles, stories and visual material. Among the staff we would especially like to thank Andrew Timpson, John Seaman and Peter Poore for writing chapter commentaries and for other contributions. In addition, we acknowledge Mark Bowden's work on the Introduction.

We also acknowledge the valuable assistance of the Overseas Development Institute, in particular the contributions of John Howell, its Director, Michèle Low and Nidhi Tandon.

General references to 'Africa' in this book are to sub-Saharan Africa, which excludes the North African Maghreb countries and South Africa. Quotations from the UN Convention on the Rights of the Child which appear in the text are taken from the summary of the Convention (see Appendix).

Thanks are due to Maureen Seely for picture research. The publishers would also like to thank the following for permission to reproduce copyright photographs (the references are to page numbers):

Martin Barasa: 98, 99; Ian Berry: 33, 34; Mark Bowden: 32; Colin Scott: 78; Peter Charlesworth: 48, 49; Chris Eldridge: 44, 45 (top); Carlos Guarita: 15, 3 Jan Hammond: 79; Fred Kasozi: 21 (top); Jenny Matthews: 3 (bottom), 5, 11, 12, 23, 29 (bottom), 30, 43, 46 (bottom), 50, 54, 56 (top), 58, 60, 65 (bottom), 67 (top), 72, 95, 96, 105, 106, 116; Caroline Penn: 6, 10, 20, 51, 52, 53, 56 (bottom), 62 (bottom), 65 (top), 67 (bottom) 68, 69, 76, 77, 83; Liba Taylor: 4 (bottom), 46 (top), 62 (top), 66 (bottom), 89, 102; Chris Thornton: 37; Penny Tweedie: 22, 39; Mike Wells: 1, 28, 29 (top); Mike Wood: 21 (bottom). Save the Children: 66 (top), 74

Annie Allsebrook: 63; Dr J. Bindslev: 103; Associated Press: 100; Geoff Saye (OXFAM): 90, 92; John Ryle: 16; David K. Tolfree: 40; Yan Gamblin/UNICEF 3 (top), 18; Stephanie Hollyman/UNICEF: 88 (top); John Isaac/UNICEF: 4; Jorgen Schytte/UNICEF: 12 (bottom), 13; Tim Clayton/Yorkshire Evening Post 88 (bottom).

Colour plates: Carlos Guarita (Hilat Kusha); Penny Tweedie (Somalia); Mike Wells (Ethiopia); Caroline Penn (Uganda). Jenny Matthews (Ethiopia, Sudan, South Africa); Liba Taylor (Zimbabwe, Lesotho); Caroline Penn (Gambia). Ne Cooper and Jan Hammond (Tanzania); Caroline Penn (Uganda); Peter Charlesworth (Burkina Faso); Jenny Matthews (Mozambique); Liba Taylor (Zimbabwe, Lesotho); Caroline Penn (Uganda); Jenny Matthews (Mozambiqu South Africa).

Christian Aid/Ian Berry

The Save the Children Fund would like to express its appreciation for the financial support received from IBM United Kingdom Trust for the preparation of this book.

Introduction by the Africa Review Group

'When we talk about the Rights of the Child, we must concern ourselves first and foremost with the child's basic rights – the right to life, the right to health and the right to a basic education. Our duty is first to secure these rights, which in other developed countries are taken for granted.

'Children cannot speak for themselves. And yet when we adults make mistakes, they are the group that suffers most from our mistakes.

'Time was, in traditional African society, when the well-being of a child was the responsibility of every adult in the community. We must revive that sense of communal responsibility.'

President Museveni of Uganda, November 1988

Two years ago, in a book called *Prospects for Africa*, the Save the Children Fund drew attention to the serious economic situation in sub-Saharan Africa and its consequences for African families. In particular the book highlighted three main concerns: debt, population and health, and the drylands. It pointed out that more international aid and investment in Africa was essential to make up for severe losses in export production and foreign exchange earnings and the resulting inability to carry out programmes necessary for survival and development.

This new book focuses on the situation of children and families in need in Africa. In doing so it has not overlooked the international economic climate but has concentrated on the community and especially on the vulnerability of the child. The publication of the first UN Convention on the Rights of the Child (see appendix, page 119) provides an opportunity to reflect both on the glaring injustice which thwart the survival and health of children, and on the range of efforts which are being made on their behalf.

As was shown in the previous book, voluntary agencies like Save the Children are making a significant contribution in Africa. The stories and evidence received from the field provide vivid example of the struggle of Africa's children and their families and friends to attain a decent, healthy and, as far as possible, peaceful life.

Save the Children have four reasons for presenting this evidence now. First, to illustrate some of the basic rights which are being denied to children and which should be upheld. Second, to show where and how children and their families in Africa are under threat. Third, to demonstrate the support which children are already receiving from the local community, from health workers and other skilled staff of aid agencies, and from government. Finally, to suggest some of the important areas in which governments and aid organisations can make their contribution.

The UN Convention has come at the end of a decade of almost unrelenting hardship for millions of children on the African continent. Nearly half of the population in sub-Saharan Africa comprises children, yet these children have had to endure an economic decline in Africa which has threatened the very structure which have been painfully created to protect and support them.

The right to survival is central to any discussion of children's rights. The new Convention recognises that 'every child has the inherent right to life' and that the survival and development of the child should be ensured 'to the maximum extent possible'. Furthermore, the Convention recognises in its preamble that the family is 'the fundamental group' of society and 'the natural environment for the growth and the well-being of all its members and particularly children'.

The decline in Africa's economic circumstances has brought change to African family life and weakened the capacity of the family to support and sustain its children. Other factors such as conflict and emergencies have increasingly weakened the poorer families in the continent. At a national level, the reduced budgets of many African countries has meant that the state has been able to provide fewer resources for health, education and other programmes which safeguard a child's right to survival and development.

The evidence in this book gives some idea of the scale of the problems facing children in certain African countries. The demand made on Africa's social workers and health personnel are enormous – many more than dwindling government budgets can support. The work of foreign-based voluntary agencies is limited in its scope and geographical area. By far the greatest burden falls on government services, both national and regional, with the resources only partly provided by the international aid community.

The world's media have tended to play down the achievements African governments in providing services and meeting human needs. In fact, as was shown in the earlier book, the record of some African governments in health and education has been remarkable when measured against the historical background and the available resources. In outlining the various needs of children this book looks carefully at the question of funding and managing social and health services at the local level and at the 'sustainability' of programmes in the future, and it tries to identify some of the key issues which need to be addressed.

Conflict and apartheid

The economic instability of recent years has been, perhaps more than ever, worsened by civil conflict and natural disaster. A handful of stories of children caught up in gruesome battles, and even recruited for them, are enough evidence of the destruction of young lives which is going on day after day. Humanitarian agencies and the churches may play a mediating role, but they are powerless to prevent conflict; they mainly have to cope with its effects.

In Southern Africa there have been encouraging moves towards peace, and some change has taken place in South Africa itself. But the scale of suffering which has occurred throughout this region cannot simply be laid at the door of ethnic or ideological rivalry: it has been encouraged and supported by a minority regime, condemned by the whole world.

The concern of specialised voluntary agencies like SCF is that, in addition to the suffering caused by the conflict in Southern Africa, wars in Africa in general have become more destructive. The growing use of sophisticated weapons in countries like Ethiopia, Sudan and Uganda have posed a greater threat to non-combatants, especially vulnerable groups such as children, than ever before. This is turn takes an enormous toll on the resources which such agencies, in partnership with governments, are able to supply.

Preparation for emergencies

Emergencies in Africa have had a major impact on child survival. Famines have killed millions of children. Yet many African governments have not had the capacity both to deal with the emergency problems facing them and to invest sufficient resources in transport and other infrastructure which would in turn help to strengthen the country's capacity to deal with such emergencies.

A carefully planned investment in roads, for example, will help to mitigate the effects of disaster, but it would also have a long-term developmental impact. Furthermore, emergency assistance can be of far greater value if it is designed to help strengthen the long-term economic potential of the country as a whole.

The current emphasis by aid agencies and governments on early warning systems should also be redirected, not just to the question of detecting drought or crop failure but to ways in which the local economy can be strengthened and in which emergency relief can be made more sensitive to the needs of the farmer.

Health: a key to development

Infectious diseases and malnutrition are by far the most serious threats to an African child's survival. Child mortality in Africa is still alarmingly high, and rising again in some countries. Burkina Faso, Mali, Ethiopia and Malawi are among those with the highest infant mortality rates in the world. The UN Convention recognises the child's right to 'the enjoyment of the highest attainable standard of health and to facilities for the treatment of illness and rehabilitation of health'. In particular, the Convention urges signatories to 'combat disease and malnutrition within the framework of primary health care through the application of readily available technology and through the provision of adequate nutritious foods and clean drinking water'.

Adequate nutrition and understanding of food and hygiene are essential to the health of the family, especially mothers and small children. But they are only part of the solution to a much wider problem. Health is often proportional to the standard of living which prevails in the surrounding community. Rural development and greater self-reliance in staple foods are also necessary, to boost local incomes and to complement actions taken at a household level. Small-scale projects such as well-digging, irrigation and sanitation schemes, even if they require outside resources, bring their own returns in community health and economic prosperity.

In recent years, we have seen the development of simple appropriate health technologies which can influence the pattern of disease in developing countries. But the capacity of many governments in Africa to support and sustain these services has diminished. The dilemma facing most ministries of health in Africa is how to use limited budgets to provide the most effective health services. If we are to see the development of adequate health care in Africa, there needs to be a considerable long-term investment by governments in this sector.

It is a myth that primary health care is cheap and affordable; even basic services require substantial investment. The training and support of health personnel is expensive. Often retraining is required to help people to be effective and motivated in their work. Salaries have to be paid. Money is needed to maintain health centres and essential drugs must be paid for in hard-earned foreign exchange.

Some African governments are examining ways in which health services can be sustained, at least partly, from local resources. The 'Bamako Initiative', signed by many African countries, has sought to encourage the recovery of part of the non-salary costs of health care through user charges – for instance, revolving fund schemes to cover the purchase of drugs. However, such schemes make a very small contribution to the overall cost of health programmes.

The bulk of external aid to Africa has been for infrastructure (especially power and energy) and production (especially agricultural exports). Mostly donor countries do not consider health care crucial enough to national economic development to warrant large-scale assistance. Economic 'adjustment' means that health budgets are frequently the first to suffer; but this is an inverted priority. Poor health leads to uneconomic performance. If children have the right to a reasonable standard of health and if government is to improve the quality of life for the whole of the population, basic health services will require the same sort of commitment from government as other sectors.

Arguably, the most serious and elusive public health hazard in Africa today is the spread of the human immunodeficiency virus which causes AIDS. In certain countries public awareness of this emergency is high, and some selective control is being carried out. But much more research is needed, and until a reliable method of control can be devised, thousands more Africans will die. The best that most people with AIDS can hope for today is the care given by their own families.

The family environment

The UN Convention states that the family is the natural environment for the growth and well-being of all its members. But economic pressures of recent years have done much to disrupt traditional family life and, increasingly, the rural population have been forced to enter the 'cash economy'. The demand for more cash income has meant that children have been encouraged to move into paid employment at an early age. The lure of the town has also done much to disrupt the family and to draw children into an area of seemingly high opportunity.

Economic recession has in many cases seriously undermined the extended family structure, making children even more vulnerable. In South Africa, the migrant labour system already divides families for long periods. High rates of unemployment there and elsewhere have meant that the male members of the family are increasingly forced to stay at home while women have had to find work in the domestic sector or in light industry, at barely subsistence levels of earnings.

Children are frequently cared for by people other than parents, and inadequate parental control and supervision is a serious cause of concern for society. During a recession, the most vulnerable face the most risk. The disabled child becomes an added responsibility for the family because he or she not only requires more attention, but also suffers more from being unable to contribute at an early age to the cash needs of the family.

The problems of war, conflict and famine in Africa have also taken their toll on the family. Inevitably, in an emergency children become separated from parents and fathers leave their families to look for employment or to try and find food. In Ethiopia such disruption was on a massive scale and thousands of young children became separated from their families. In Uganda and Mozambique, too, many families have been divided and children left to themselves have suffered harrowing experiences.

While the ultimate answer may lie in solving the economic and political problems of the continent, a great deal can be done immediately to improve both the law and the services which support the family and the child.

Strengthening social services

In most African countries, social services are even more severely stretched than health services, and are often more neglected. Little training is available for social workers, and consequently the services offered are based mostly on outdated European models. If social services in Africa could be adapted to strengthen support to the family, they could be extremely effective.

The legal framework under which families and children currentl live is often inappropriate. Legal adoption and fostering are usuall lengthy and difficult processes and little financial assistance is available to settle a child within the family. Poor institutional care most frequently the only option available to the displaced or abandoned child. Yet in Africa the institution should really be the last resort. In a continent where the extended family is still strong our efforts should be devoted to strengthening that framework rather than creating an alternative.

The problem of street children and young offenders can also be much alleviated through the process of judicial reform and review Little is currently available to help such children. Very few countri in Africa have members of the judiciary that are actively involved responsible for juvenile and child offenders, and the police or soci services may have no alternative but to use penal institutions.

The educational challenge

A child's right to education is fundamental. This is recognised in t UN Convention which recommends that primary education shou be 'compulsory and available free to all'. Governments should encourage the development of secondary and higher education, 'making them available and accessible to every child'.

It is not going to be easy to implement these rights in the Africa the 1990s. In some countries the opportunity still does not exist. Mozambique for example, the lack of suitably trained and qualifi teachers is a severe block to development.

Kenya, on the other hand, has large numbers of children who have completed secondary education and are unable to find employment. In this case secondary education, which is frequently seen as a means to escape poverty, has instead inspired only frustrated expectations. Such children from poor rural backgrounds have drifted to the shanty towns of Nairobi and in some cases resorted to crime in order to repay their parents' investment in education.

Throughout Africa universal primary education and the extension of adult literacy are among the highest priorities. In the 1970s primary education for all appeared to be within the reach of most African countries. However the last decade has seen this achievement whittled away as investment has been unable to keep up with the demand for education. Economic decline has also had an immediate impact on many families' capacity to support their children through education. Increasingly children who might have gone to school in better times are kept at home. There are also considerable pressures on children which stop them from completing their education.

There are ways in which children can be helped both to enter and to remain in the education system. In some countries, school feeding schemes have enabled children to stay in education by helping to reduce the economic burden on the family. The provision of education in Africa needs to be more flexible, allowing children to drop in and out of the system. The education of girls is now receiving more emphasis in some African countries and this trend needs to be maintained.

Such measures require investment, and philosophies that espouse cost recovery locally penalise the already disadvantaged. In this instance education is not like health. Faced with increased costs and more pressure on limited family resources, children will opt out of schooling. The investment that is needed is not merely to help governments extend and improve the education system as a whole, but also to provide the support required to allow disadvantaged children the same access to education as others already enjoy.

According to Uganda's President Museveni: 'Time was, in traditional African society, when the well-being of a child was the responsibility of every adult in the community. We must revive that sense of communal responsibility.' The African family is one of the continent's great strengths. It is foolish to see development as a mainly economic process. Aid from outside can and should also be used to support the fabric of society. Currently there is little evidence of this anywhere in Africa, and yet much can be done with relatively modest finances.

At the end of this book there are offered a number of specific conclusions and recommendations. But the involvement of experts needs to be matched by greater awareness on the part of the public, especially those who are concerned about Africa and already support aid organisations. We are certain that this book, and the first hand evidence it contains, will contribute in some way towards this wider understanding of the problems and prospects facing Africa's children.

Many situations of conflict and poverty, for which we are proposing particular immediate solutions, belong to a wider economic and political pattern for which the governments of Brit. and other industrialised countries, as well as the governments of Africa, all bear responsibility. There must be a renewed effort towards international economic and political solutions, and all of should play a part in tackling the wider problems which affect children. At the same time we need to give energetic and enthusias support to international and national voluntary agencies which a campaigning and working so actively on behalf of children.

HRH The Princess Royal
President, The Save the Children Fund
Chairman, Africa Review Group

Chief Emeka Anyaoku
Commonwealth Secretary-General Designate

The Rt Revd Simon Barrington Ward
Bishop of Coventry

Ms Brenda Dean
General Secretary, Society of Graphical and Allied Trades

Mr Jonathan Dimbleby
Broadcaster and journalist

Mr Derk Pelly
Former Deputy Chairman, Barclays Bank

Baroness Young
Former Minister of State at the Foreign Office

CHILD VICTIMS
OF WAR AND
VIOLENCE

Child Victims of War and Violence

The dark brought its own sense of fear for the children. The transient peace of the night was wrenched away by the breaking down of doors and of screaming. The off-duty soldiers had come again on another looting party. These raiding parties were occasions of uncertainty. Had they come to steal, to kill or to abduct the children? The soldiers themselves had been afraid: they had guns and pangas, but the security of did not always overcome their own fears. In the end, the strength of the group had won and a night of brutal violence had begun again.

Childhood is often fraught with fear. It is only the love and security of the family and friends which provide reassurance. During conflict, the family is rendered fragile. It is often destroyed by conflict itself and by the corollaries of violence: the escape to refugee camps; the destruction of the home and the degradation of the land. More damaging, perhaps, is the destruction of culture, of social norms of behaviour.

The Save the Children Fund (SCF) was born early in this century at a time of war in Europe. Within the last decade in Africa, SCF ha become increasingly involved in war zones and areas of conflict. This has usually meant that it has provided medical and nutritiona care to children who have been denied access to any services. More recently this care has been extended to offering protection to children – a role normally carried out by the International Red Cross. Unfortunately the Red Cross's ability to supervise the Gene Convention has been severely constrained. Its delegates are often asked to leave a country or are forbidden to enter an area where there is a conflict. Furthermore, many governments deny that there is a conflict within their frontiers, often referring to banditry or hooliganism when the reality is outright civil war.

SCF's experience in Africa bears witness to an unrelenting tragedy. Within the past decade we have seen mass starvation in northern Ethiopia and southern Sudan. Brutal internecine wars in Somalia, Mozambique, Uganda and Angola have resulted in the cynical degradation of children's lives. In regions where food and medicines are in short supply, Kalashnikov rifles are in abundance and dictate social life. In another, much wealthier, part of Africa, children have been at the mercy of armoured cars and tear gas.

Children appear to have many enemies in countries like Sudan and Mozambique. They are special targets to the combatants, who realise that an effective way to destroy a community's resolve in opposing a government, a party or a movement is by attacking the most vulnerable part – the children.

Uganda – shattered homes, Masuliita

Mozambique *Children under attack*

Miguel

'I'm 12 and I've been here for three months. I'm here because of the bandits. They came into my village near Pebane and started attacking people. They destroyed my school, so we had to run away and we managed to get to a boat and come down to Quelimane. It took a couple of days. My mother and father had both died: my mother lost her legs when she stepped on a mine, then the stump got infected and she died. My father died of tuberculosis. I ran away with my little brother Victorinho. When we first came here we lived on the street, asking people for food, but then we were picked up and sent here to the orphanage. My hopes are to be able to study and to grow up. I don't quite know what the future will be like.

'When I was in my village I used to worry about the war a lot. We were always afraid of being attacked by the bandits, but here in Quelimane I feel much safer. Life in the orphanage is quite good. I've got friends here, I can go to school and we get meals every day – lunch and supper. Before it was a problem for us to get enough to eat. Also we can get washed here, there's water in the building, we don't have to walk a long way to fetch it. I don't mind staying here. Accion Social (the social services) have been trying to find a family for me here in Quelimane – I hope they do.'

Adolfo

'I'm 12 years old. At the moment I'm in Alto Moloque because the armed bandits came and attacked my town, Ile. I'm here by myself because I got cut off from my family and they had to stay behind. I don't know what has happened to them, or if I'll see them again. I just followed the other people walking through the bushes until we got here.'

Buenaventura

'I'm 13 and was in the 5th class at school in Ile. On February 16th the enemy came into our district early in the morning. I ran away with my father – we walked here. The journey was sad because several people died on the way – mostly little babies. It was raining all the time and it was difficult to walk, we had to cross deep rivers and some children drowned. There was nothing to eat and some people died from hunger too. Now I'm sad because we've lost our home, friends have disappeared and I don't know what's going to happen to us.'

Jaime

'I'm 14 and from Ile. We had to come here because the armed bandits came into town. I ran away with my family – my mother, my father and three brothers and sisters. It was a terrible journey, it poured with rain, we had nothing to eat and it took us three days to get here. We walked in a long line, one after the other, each person

Jenny Matthews photographed and interviewed these children in orphanages in Quelimane and Alto Moloque, Zambezia province, in March 1989.

just carrying what they had time to pick up. Some women carried cooking pots on their heads and children in their arms. I brought r guitar. We had to leave some old and sick people behind. It's hard go back for them because there's no road, you just have to walk through the bush.'

Adolfo

Buenaventura

Jaime

Traumatised children

The psychological damage caused by displacement and conflict is always difficult to estimate. Individual trauma often gets overshadowed by mass misery, but the damage done to children in conflict is inevitably tragic, and irrevocable in its effect on the way that the child views the adult world.

The report which follows, which includes interviews with children, describes the experience that many children have endured during the war in Mozambique. The report is based on an SCF study, concluded in 1988, by a team which included Dr Pam Zinkin, Dr Naomi Richman and Nazneen Kanji from the Institute of Child Health in London.

Since 1979, Mozambique has had little respite from guerilla war. Externally supported armed bands of terrorists, the so-called Mozambique National Resistance (MNR), have been carrying out policy of deliberate destruction of schools, health posts and factories. They burn houses and crops, murder, rape and loot. Ove two million people have been displaced from their homes, thousands of children have been orphaned, and many children hav been kidnapped.

This continuing terrorism produces a range of traumatising experiences for Mozambican children. They include hunger and illness, disability, displacement, separation and bereavement, violence and sexual abuse, witnessing violence against members of their own families, and direct participation in violence.

There is a deliberate policy of training boys to take part in violer attacks. After they are captured, they are starved and beaten and threatened with death if they do not obey. They see enough brutali to know these threats will be carried out. They spend long hours 'training' and drilling, and may go on to learn how to use arms and how to shoot and kill. They may be forced to kill animals to get use to the sight of blood.

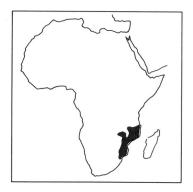

Mozambique – lives to be rebuilt

Angelino

Angelino, from Maringwe, was 11 when his family were forced to leave their village when the MNR attacked. Two of his brothers died during the fight. Over the next few years he experienced five more attacks, during which some of his schoolmates were killed including his best friend. Eventually he fled to Malawi with his parents but was unable to study, so at the age of 16 he returned to Mozambique to attend a residential school near Beira.

Amelia

Twelve-year-old Amelia, from Chibabane, saw both her parents bayoneted to death by the MNR. Her mother was pregnant at the time. Amelia tried to run away but was shot in the head. She was in hospital for six months and was then transferred to an orphanage. There the staff found that she was restless and could not concentrate, she cried a great deal and complained of pains in her head and body. She talked continuously about her parents' death.

When interviewed Amelia sat on the paediatrician's knee and said, 'I am not well'. She spoke without emotion. 'I'm alone. I have no father. I have no mother. The bandits killed my parents. I've got a pain in my head. I was shot in the head. I get attacks. I get frightened.'

Paulo

Paulo, also aged 12, was playing with his friends when the terrorists started shooting at them. Some managed to run away, some were killed but Paulo and a few of his friends were captured. They were forced to walk for two days without food. When they arrived at the MNR base they were separated and Paulo never saw his friends again. He was kept as a slave, beaten daily, and was only given green leaves to eat. After a month he managed to escape and was reunited with his parents. Sadly, the whereabouts of his two brothers, kidnapped previously by the MNR, were still unknown.

Joaquim

Joaquim is a young boy of about 11 from Caia district. Both his parents were killed by the MNR and he was captured. When he tried to escape he was caught, beaten and tied up for a week. He knew that if he had been an adult he would have been killed. Thus he was forced to begin military training. He learnt how to kill, but it is not certain if he killed anyone. Eventually he managed to escape while collecting water.

When brought to an orphanage, Joaquim was suffering from severe malnutrition. He was agitated and difficult to control, frequently running away, but returning. He was aggressive, jolting other children and smoking cannabis and cigarettes whenever he could. When interviewed he looked thoughtful and sad but was responding to the care given him in the orphanage.

Mozambique – simulation game

Thousands of children have suffered physically and psychologically from horrifying experiences in Mozambique. Many have found their way into camps, temporary settlements and orphanages.

Primary school teachers, although themselves victims of MNR attacks, continue to work with the children under the most difficult conditions, helping them to learn and providing comfort however they can. Families, already short of food and clothing, try to help the orphaned children and to share what they have.

SCF, among other agencies, supports Mozambican government and community efforts to resettle the children in families (see page 72), although it is not easy to reach all affected children.

 In Abyei in southern Sudan, during 1988, 6000 children starved to death or died of diseases caused by malnutrition. This appeared to be the result of a wilful policy of neglect by local officials as aid could have reached Abyei in time, but obstacles were put in the way of agencies bringing food and medical care. Of course, the children concerned were Dinka, and were thus seen as future recruits for the 'rebel' Sudan People's Liberation Movement. Nevertheless, callous denial of help to such children does not always destroy the support for a political movement: in fact, it can strengthen it.

Sudan

Travelling to survive

Chris Thornton, an Assistant Field Director for SCF in East Africa, tells this story of a Dinka family from Southern Sudan.

Atak Atong

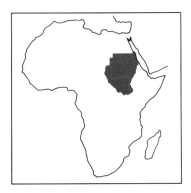

Atak Atong is a sturdy, athletic boy of about eight. He's a good-looking lad and his smooth face knows how to smile. But his eyes tell you that he also takes life pretty seriously.

In a group of twenty chattering children Atak's comments rise above the hubbub, not bossily, but with a casual authority. In a fix, Atak would be the type of guy to stick close to.

He lives now in a settlement by a village called El Ligam, in the South Darfur region of western Sudan. He shares a 'tukul' or hut with his father, mother and younger sister. His uncle and aunt and three cousins have a tukul next door.

His family are Dinkas. They used to live in Nyamlell, near Awiel, in the Bahr el Ghazal region. Atak ought to be the third in a line of six children. Instead he is the elder of just two; the other four brothers and sisters are now mere statistics, evidence of the high death rate from disease among children in Sudan. Atak shrugs when he mentions his family.

In early 1988 they had to leave Nyamlell. The village was attacked on several occasions by roving militias from the north. Animals were stolen, crops burnt and people shot. Some villagers were taken away by the gangs – men and boys to work the land, women and girls to work in their homes. Then there was a drought which left them without food. And having no animals to sell they couldn't buy food. Even if they had money there was often nothing in the market because the militias closed the roads and stopped the movement of goods. Destitute and with no alternative, Atak's

family left home and headed north to where they knew there would be food.

'We walked for two days,' Atak recalls. 'It was very hard for me because I am small. My legs swelled up. My mother carried my sister. All we had with us was a water container. We slept in the open and ate a meal of cooked leaves from the "thau" tree.

'We crossed the Bahr el Arab river and arrived at Sefaha where we found some Europeans giving out groundnuts, grain and oil. We stayed there for a while and then came by truck to El Ligam.'

Altogether 16,000 Dinka people were moved from Sefaha and set up in seven settlements sited near Arab villages in South Darfur. It was arranged jointly by the regional government, the host villages, the Dinkas and three foreign non-government organisations: Save the Children, Oxfam and Médecins Sans Frontières (Belgium).

'When we arrived at El Ligam,' says Atak, 'we were given some oil and groundnuts and a bag of durra (sorghum grain). We were also given a jerry can with water and a plastic sheet. We cut some wood and some millet stalks to build ourselves a tukul.'

Atak remembers how, back in Nyamlell, he helped his father with the farming. During the day, in the rainy season, he worked in the fields. Using a hoe he dug a line of holes. Then he went down the line throwing in one or two seeds of durra, sesame or millet. Then he covered each hole. When the time came he helped with the weeding and also with the harvest.

'In the evening I used to corral the sheep and goats in a "lwok" (barn). I used to light fires around them to make smoke to keep away the insects and their diseases.'

In his short life Atak hasn't had much chance to develop any interests beyond home and work. He did go to school for a month in a village near Nyamlell, but had to stop because the militias were around and it was unsafe.

He may be able to go to school in El Ligam, but there is a problem. The local Arab villagers are still building the school, adding new classes each year, and there isn't yet room for all the village children, let alone the settlers. The hope is that Save the Children will build more classrooms and make desks and benches too.

The increased demand on village resources as a result of the influx of southerners applies even more critically to water. In the dry season each year, from January onwards, this intensifies. Firstly, the water table falls. Secondly, more southerners are likely to flee north. Thirdly, Arab herders return from northern grazing lands to their Darfur villages, bringing thousands of thirsty animals with them.

The 'Omdas', the village head men, are worried that the competition for water may upset the spirit of co-operation that now exists between villagers and settlers, despite generations of traditional enmity. In neighbouring Kordofan, thousands of Dinkas were abandoned to their fate and starved to death.

Aware of these underlying tensions, relief organisers are determined that the programme's benefits should go to settlers and villagers alike. Oxfam have repaired boreholes and have put in multiple stand-pipes to improve village water supplies and protect their cleanliness.

Atak is sensitive to the fragile political balancing act that enables him to stay in El Ligam. All the children are on edge after the recent night raids and he speaks for them all when he says: 'I did like it here but now people attack, and if they continue to attack I won't like it any more.'

In the end, Atak would rather go home to Nyamlell where he imagines himself growing up, marrying and moving into his own tukul. 'If there is food again in the south and if the northerners stop attacking, then we will go back; but not before.'

Sudan – runaway slaves, South Kordofan

There have been convincing reports of a revival of slavery in parts of southern and western Sudan. Many Dinka women and children have been taken hostage by raiding pro-government militias. Some of these children have remained in bondage and been made to work for local farmers, and girls have sometimes been forced into concubinage.

According to the Anti-Slavery Society, the market price of child slaves in Sudan has fallen rapidly as more children have become available. 'At the beginning of 1988, prices of children averaged £60; by March that had halved to £30; and it is thought now to be around £10 – so one automatic weapon equals in value six or seven slaves.'

Children are counted with the enemy in all wars, and sometimes they become 'the' enemy. In low-intensity conflict, the actual combatants suffer few casualties and the victims are often children. Attacking the vulnerable is, of course, not new. Europe's contact with Africa was partly based on such a premise, but African leaders and soldiers have learned these techniques too. To corral people together in times of war, to deny them health services and food deliveries: this is the way to defeat and subject people.

Between 1981 and 1986, Uganda fought one of the ugliest civil wars the modern world has witnessed. The National Resistance Army (NRA) under Yoweri Museveni was fighting the government of Milton Obote, challenging a faulty election process. Much of this war was fought in a densely forested area north of Kampala called the 'Luwero Triangle'. Unable to draw the guerillas into combat, the government decided to terrorise the local inhabitants.

A system of concentration camps was set up by the government. Villages were emptied of their inhabitants and a free fire zone was created. People not living in the camps were considered to be 'bandits' and could be shot on sight.

The most devastating action by the government was the withdrawal of all services. Social services collapsed in this prosperous area and the army went on a looting spree in such a comprehensive way that no building within the Triangle had its roof intact. Cattle, grain and coffee were stolen by the army so that the population became utterly destitute and were reduced to going on gathering forays to collect cassava.

Under these conditions, the mortality rate among children was exceptionally high. A measles epidemic caused hundreds of child deaths in one camp and malnutrition slowly took its toll among the under-fives. Children were not adequately protected. Young girls were abducted by the soldiers and became concubines. There were numerous instances of multiple rape. Adolescent boys were often killed as they were always seen as potential rebels.

It was under these circumstances that many children fled and joined Museveni in the bush. The NRA became a cohesive guerrilla force with a considerable number of child soldiers, and in many ways the army as an institution became the parent of these children.

*U*ganda

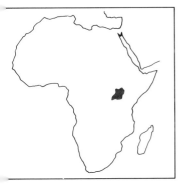

Children in the Luwero Triangle

Ita Riley was in charge of feeding programmes in the Luwero Triangle run jointly by SCF, Oxfam and the Red Cross in 1983–84. She returned to Uganda in 1986–88 to work on nutritional surveys in Luwero and two other districts.

We got involved in Luwero after two of our staff went there in a Land Rover one day early in 1983. Half an hour out of Kampala they came across clusters of people, some being forcibly moved into camps by Obote's soldiers. Most were accused of supporting Museveni's guerrillas. Others were going of their own free will because they were frightened of being attacked and raped in their own homes.

The Triangle encompassed three districts and soldiers were scattered throughout the area. To reach one feeding centre we had to travel through 15 road-blocks. Soldiers were often based in these camps and severely restricted the movements of the people. This inevitably had an adverse effect on food distribution.

Despite reassurances that they would be protected in these camps, people's lives were often in jeopardy. Women were raped by the soldiers, and men suspected of guerrilla activity were taken out of the camps at night and murdered. Only later on, after Museveni became president, it was realised that tens of thousands had been killed.

In a lot of these camps we set up feeding centres. We never had any formal permission to work in the area and as time went on it became increasingly difficult to reach the camps as the army placed more restrictions on our movements. By the end of my time they had stopped the Red Cross, but would occasionally allow SCF or Oxfam vehicles to pass. We were only taking supplementary food for the children and because there wasn't a regular supply of food for adults the effectiveness of our programme was questionable.

There was no real authority other than the military in the camps and this often caused a great deal of confusion and unpleasantness. At times we were threatened by drunken soldiers waving their guns at us, which was a little worrying and hard to cope with.

Battles were going on all the time outside the camps. The Luwero Triangle is a very bushy area, ideal for guerrilla warfare. We didn't

see wounded on a large scale because the fighting wasn't actually in the camps, where the large majority were women and children. But years later, piles of male corpses were found not far from these camps.

In one village the nephew of a health visitor was seriously wounded. He needed to receive medical attention in Kampala if he was to survive. After discussion we decided to take the risk. This meant a three and a half hour journey through the road blocks. It wasn't until we set out that we realised just how dangerous the journey was for us as he could so easily have been taken for one of Museveni's men. However, despite one or two worrying moments, we returned safely to the city and happily the nephew made a full recovery from his bullet wounds.

We often came across children who had been orphaned or separated from their parents. At times we were responsible for splitting up families. If one child in the family was severely malnourished he or she often needed intensive feeding in Kampala. This inevitably meant that we would take one child with another family member as a guardian, leaving the rest of the family behind. Once the child had recovered, the aim was then to return the pair to the family.

At the end of the war many children were moved into children's homes in Kampala. The Red Cross looked after the adults and SCF took responsibility for the children. Not all the children were orphans and SCF social workers started to look for the families of the displaced children.

The picture was often confusing because some mothers who had lost their husbands in the war had remarried and moved elsewhere. Not all 'new' husbands wanted or were able to take on the extra burden of their wives' children. At times, when their parents were traced, children did not want to return home, having grown used to city life and feeling estranged from their families. In other cases, parents felt their children were better off in the homes and were often receiving a good education which was unavailable in the villages.

After returning to Uganda two years later I was initially responsible for work in these children's homes, working closely wit social workers and health visitors. War and its aftermath have a crippling effect on family life in any country, and Uganda was a prime example. The aspect which disturbed me more than any othe was the damage it had done to the traditional African extended family.

In the West we have always admired the African commitment to family life, seeing in our 'developed' society nuclear families that would benefit from extended family support. Unfortunately, due to the number of years of war in Uganda, many families have lost this commitment and understandably life for many communities has become the survival of the fittest.

Outside resources should not be swallowed up, as some are, in reinforcing some parents' misconceptions that children's homes offer a better lifestyle than their own. They should rather be used to help rural families to realise their own strengths in providing a safe caring environment for their children.

The aftermath of conflict, whether defeat or liberation, is both chaotic and traumatic. Families are often long displaced from their homes and separated through conflict and a slow, painful process of reunification and rehabilitation has to begin. Disability becomes a more prominent problem. In the streets of Port Sudan, there are teenagers who have lost limbs, and they are only the visible cost of the Eritrean conflict.

SCF has developed considerable expertise in helping children retrace their parents and relatives. It is a humane approach, following the view that the family is normally a safer refuge than the institution (see also chapters two and four).

> Fred Kasozi, an experienced Ugandan social worker with SCF, describes the frustrating but often rewarding task of tracing families of unaccompanied children.

After the war in Uganda, we started a tracing service to locate the families of children who had ended up in orphanages in and around Kampala. We knew it was not enough to relieve their physical pain and that their mental suffering, caused by the uncertainty of the fate of those families, was equally cruel.

It was not easy to get information from children that had seen their parents shot, burnt or buried alive. We went through some very taxing interviews. Once we had established a relationship with these children they told us a lot which could not even be summarised here.

The roads in the Luwero Triangle, where we have been doing most of our tracing work, have been in a shambles. From time to time our vehicles break down because the tracks have deep ruts and are impassable. At times we return without finding anyone. Essential services are still lacking in many places and it will be years before people come back to live there; wild animals like pigs and monkeys are still harassing any food that is grown. In other places, a lot of people have returned to their homes but they still need resettlement assistance.

Waswa and Kityo

Waswa and Kityo are two brothers who in 1983 were aged 12 and 8. They came from around Masuliita in Mpigi District, an area which suffered more than most during the war. They lived with their parents, an elder brother called Kaggwa, and a younger one called Bysansi.

The war in that districted started in Waswa's school, when soldiers invaded it, thinking it was harbouring guerrillas. The war then spread all over the area. Waswa and his family ran away from the village after hearing several shots. Unfortunately they ran in different directions. Waswa said most of them ran to a place in the Singo area, 70 miles away, but by the time they arrived, their mother and youngest brother were already missing. They spent some time in a camp and then ran further to Kiboga until their father became ill and weak and eventually died.

Waswa and his brother Kityo were picked up by the Red Cross team and brought to Mulago, very sick and malnourished. They received treatment and were later moved to an orphanage in

Kampala. Waswa went to the Polytechnic School in Jinja along with nine other boys who got training in carpentry and tailoring.

After a year we arranged a tracing visit to the area of Masuliita, taking a group of ten boys including Waswa and Kityo. It was a tedious, gruelling journey through ditches and thick swamps. Waswa took one look at Masuliita and his old school, and he felt as if he was dreaming. He recognised the area, but he was not sure whether he would find anybody in his home village, five kilometres from Masuliita town.

We found an escort to direct us to the place. The roads were almost impassable. In some places we had to walk ahead along the track, trying to spot hidden ditches and huge stumps under the thick grass.

When we got there we found that the house itself had been burnt down, but the boys recognised their elder brother Kaggwa, and many other relatives and village friends who could not believe that Waswa and Kityo were still alive. I wish I had had a video recorder. The excitement and congratulations were mixed with tears as they all told their sad stories. We were left in a state of utter confusion. In turn, Waswa and his younger brother told their relatives all that had happened to them. Eventually we left the place because it was getting dark.

Waswa returned to Jinja and after some months he completed his tailoring course, after which SCF helped him to resettle in Masuliita with a sewing machine. In February 1988, he was honoured to meet HRH The Princess Royal, during her visit to Uganda. After a few months Kityo also moved out of the orphanage, and was able to join his family.

Kityo and his younger brother now go to Masuliita primary school which SCF has also helped to rehabilitate. Their elder brother is now the head of the family; the youngest brother, Byansi, still looks a bit weak and somewhat deformed.

All these events were part of the price of Uganda's war. The children lost both their parents and some other relatives. They lost their possessions and were socially and psychologically affected. Today, when you ask them how they are, or try to observe them in their happiest mood, it is very hard to believe that they are really happy. Perhaps it costs them a lot to smile. What is more apparent is the mood of sadness and the lack of hope for a better future. Our professional support to encourage them to become self-reliant is still continuing.

Joseph Luwero

Among some very young unaccompanied children who were brought from the camps to the new Mulago hospital, I was alerted to one eight-month-old baby who had been admitted to ward 3C with a bullet wound on his leg. One day Cardinal E K Nsubaga toured the hospital and he christened our unknown baby 'Joseph'. The child's health tremendously improved and I eventually placed him at Nsambya Babies Home. The number of caseloads on my table at that time was in the hundreds, and I had to place Joseph under an emergency procedure without a proper court order, because we were still in a war situation.

After one month Joseph's leg had completely healed but it was

Joseph in 1989

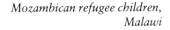

*Mozambican refugee children,
Malawi*

slightly deformed. I travelled about 60 kilometres east of Kampala to contact an old lady who had got to know Joseph at Mulago and had promised to foster him. I interviewed her, inspected her home, looked at some other children she was looking after, and I was confident that she was a suitable foster parent.

When I came back to Kampala, I waited for the woman at the agreed time and place, but she did not show up. Months elapsed until I became convinced that she had lost interest, perhaps because the tedious court procedures had put her off or scared her. Meanwhile Joseph remained at Nsambya and was given the surname 'Luwero'.

Then in 1986, an elderly lady called Nabawanga came looking for a child whose story sounded like Joseph's. I interviewed her and during the course of that interview I was made to believe that she was the maternal grandmother. She was very downcast and she told me that she had been visiting a daughter in the local hospital. But it was not the baby's mother. Sadly, she confirmed what I had already heard about Joseph. Back in 1984 his mother had gone out of the transit camp of Semuto to look for food, with Joseph on her back. Obote's soldiers saw her and shot her dead. Later one of them took the child to Mulago hospital where he was admitted as an unaccompanied baby. According to the old grandmother the baby was found suckling his dead mother's breast.

Nabawanga told me that her family was from an area south-east of Luwero. Early in 1988 I tried to trace her because I knew Joseph would soon be too big for the children's home. Children are not supposed to stay there after they are five years old. My tracing wasn't successful, but the struggle to find either Joseph's relatives or a new foster parent continues. I think it will succeed.

There are wider concerns about conflicts. Super-power rivalry in the Horn of Africa inflames internal battles in Somalia, Ethiopia and Sudan. Children become the distant casualties of American or Soviet foreign policies. Moreover, the export of chaos by the Republic of South Africa into countries like Mozambique has a direct effect on the welfare of children. Parts of Mozambique have turned into desolate areas, devoid of people, schools, clinics and trade. It is estimated by UNICEF that, between 1980 and 1988, 825,000 infants and young children died from war-related causes in Mozambique and Angola alone.

Africa is subject to enormous refugee movements, many as a direct result of open conflict. Over 755,000 Mozambicans had moved into Malawi by the end of 1989, and this number is rising. Ethiopia is host to 680,000 Sudanese and Somali refugees. Sudan itself, apart from its own displaced people, has over 650,000 refugees who have fled from the conflicts in Ethiopia. Over half of all these refugees are children (see also Chapter Two). Refugee camps are particularly bleak environments where mute poverty and disease are commonplace. Inadequate rations make life perilous for young children. The emergence of disease such as scurvy can be witnessed in refugee camps in Ethiopia, Somalia and Sudan; that children are allowed to develop this disease is scandalous.

Camps for refugees and displaced people are not necessarily a sanctuary for children. Rebel groups often operate within camps and harass and intimidate young boys so that they can be conscripted. Young girls come under threat from unscrupulous security officials. Nevertheless, even the most dire camps remain sanctuaries by comparison because at least they are outside the war area.

There are other, more insidious forms of conflict which are difficult to influence. The availability of weapons to nomadic groups, particularly in the triangle of southern Sudan, northern Uganda and northern Kenya, has started a new era of brutal cattle raiding with massive civilian casualties. The destructive effect of weapons can never be under-estimated. Tribal elders have seen their authority vitiated by well-armed teenagers who engage in reckless conflict. Children are regularly killed in these raids and the insecurity prevents the development of services.

Another serious, though little-known aspect of conflict in Africa the spread of AIDS among young people. Armies are well known a very efficient carriers of sexually transmitted diseases, including th human immunodeficiency virus (HIV).

Armed conflict occurs in many parts of Africa, and this is a majc cause of family disruption. This increases the likelihood of people having more sexual partners. Armies consist of young men who ar often far from home and friends. Sexual intercourse with several partners is more likely in these circumstances, whether as a result c rape, prostitution, comradeship or loneliness. The spoils of war usually include sexual exploitation.

In war zones there is naturally very little room for health or soci welfare. Roads and buildings are destroyed and well-trained staff flee or are killed. When adults become fearful, children lose their sense of security.

Where conflict is central to the way societies are organised, the chances for children's welfare are slim. The sources of conflict can be converted into the programmes of political parties and pressure groups; but where these groups are in the process of formation, violence becomes the inevitable corollary when a military or arme group seizes power. The welfare of children rarely fits into this scheme of government.

Africa is in a transitional stage in its history. It has been endowe with colonial institutions which are often ill-fitted to its current needs. Unfortunately, traditional methods of coping with social breakdown have been undermined by the dominance of state institutions such as children's homes, remand centres and prisons. adverse economic circumstances and in times of conflict, these institutions offer a poor service and, in fact, are often abused by governments in their dealings with troubled children.

Uganda – nurse with children

What can a small agency like SCF offer to children who are caught up in conflict? Firstly, it can offer health and nutrition services, assuming that it has access to areas where fighting is goir on. SCF's assistance to displaced or refugee children with health a feeding programmes has become a vital form of protection.

Secondly, the presence of SCF staff in an area of conflict can sometimes reduce the level of violence. They can be seen as witnesses to illegal acts. This role was useful in the Luwero Trian in Uganda, but it would be unrealistic to suggest that SCF has been able to create a 'zone of peace' within a war ravaged area.

Inevitably, SCF is often forced into a diplomatic role when the UN or Red Cross avenues have been closed. This diplomacy means advocating the protection of children who are being victimised by governments or combatants. It is a role which SCF is uneasy with. Nevertheless, it is often placed in this negotiating position, particularly in the Horn of Africa, where children's interests are badly neglected.

The new UN Convention on the Rights of the Child will be a valuable asset in the protection of children. The Convention should provide a moral imperative for all those assisting children under the threat of death, injury or serious illness. It can also provide a useful basis for negotiations between aid agencies and governments.

■ No child may be subjected to torture, degrading treatment, arbitrary arrest, life imprisonment or capital punishment. The child has a right to be treated with dignity, to be given a fair trial, and to receive legal assistance. . . .

■ No child under 15 should take direct part in armed conflict or be recruited into the armed forces, and priority in recruitment should be given to older children. The State must ensure the protection and care of children affected by armed conflict. . . .

■ A child who has been the victim of any form of neglect, abuse, torture, degrading treatment or armed conflict must be guaranteed full recovery and social reintegration in an appropriate environment. . . .

■ A child accused of breaking the law has a right to be presumed innocent until proved guilty, to receive a fair hearing, to refuse to give evidence and to have the assistance of an interpreter. The State must promote laws and procedures which specifically apply to children. . . .

From the UN Convention on the Rights of the Child

It is quite clear from SCF's experience that too many children remain inadequately protected in areas of conflict in Africa. Inevitably, the question of sovereignty arises. Outside interference is unacceptable to a government but there are universal values at play. The majority of African countries are already signatories to the Rights of the Child but many countries have ignored or neglected these responsibilities.

Sudan is a case in point. The Sudanese government has been guilty of a laissez-faire attitude to children caught up in the civil war. South Africa has had a policy of intimidating black school children by an organised and systematic process of internment and violence. This has suppressed childhood opposition to the Pretoria government and has further polarised and embittered the young black communities in the townships.

South Africa

The problems of Lucky M

These two case studies from Priscilla McKay, director of a child welfare agency in Natal supported by SCF, show how easily children and whole families can become victimised in the setting of apartheid and ethnic conflict.

Lucky

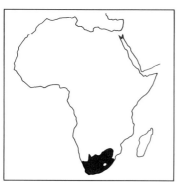

Lucky was referred to a child welfare agency when he and his 11-year-old friend were detained by the security police. His mother approached agency staff who in turn approached the police, and both children were released. Lucky was charged with attempted murder. On his release his mother said there was evidence that he had been beaten with sjamboks (whips). She said she had taken him to a doctor but was not able to produce a medical certificate.

Lucky appeared in court 11 times, but was acquitted on 12th September 1988. According to the police and his lawyer this was because the youths that he and his gang had attacked refused to give evidence in court, although they were present. According to evidence given by the police, Lucky and three friends ambushed three youths from the Inkatha Youth Brigade who were on their way to the shops and stabbed and robbed them. One youth had fled and was not found, and the other two made statements to the police which they were too afraid to corroborate in court.

When Lucky was ten years old, according to his mother, he joined the United Democratic Front – a broad-based movement, representing many organisations, which aims to challenge apartheid and bring in a democratic government. As a result Lucky became involved in the war against Inkatha, which had started a couple of years earlier in the townships in Pietermaritzburg and had then spread to other areas.

Inkatha is a movement which was revived by Chief Buthelezi in the 70s in order to give back to the Zulus a pride in their nation and a sense of tribal unity. Inkatha felt that they were losing their majority in the Natal townships, particularly among the youth, and started a forced membership drive in the townships. The UDF reacted to this and war broke out. Lucky became increasingly involved in anti-social activities and was eventually labelled a 'comtsotsi' to differentiate him from the 'comrades', who are not caught up in anti-social, negative behaviour and see themselves as fighting for causes such as equal education, the vote and the demise of apartheid. The term 'tsotsi' has been used for many years to describe a black juvenile delinquent.

Lucky was re-arrested at 4 am on 13th September 1988 and charged with armed robbery. According to the security police he had left his mother's home. His mother had had to flee after her home was petrol-bombed by Inkatha and was now living in another township.

Lucky had not settled down. He had by then returned to his friends who were living in small bands in houses vacated by their owners after threats of death or violence, having been identified as Inkatha members. These bands of youths obtain money from begging and threaten violence if people do not pay.

Once again Lucky was released to his mother, but again he left her to return to his friends. The police were looking for him. On 30th September he was admitted to hospital having been shot in the head and shoulder. The police reported that he had been shot running away from them. They said the head wound was received when he crashed a car stolen at gunpoint and was not from a gunshot. His lawyer confirmed that Lucky was again up on serious charges, that his mother could not control him, that he would be held in custody by the police until he could be transferred to a place of safety for children.

Lucky is an illegitimate child of a Coloured man and a Black woman. He looks Coloured, and according to his mother this has meant that he is easily identified in the black areas. He appears to have been rejected by his stepfather because of his colour and was initially brought up by an elderly grandmother. His mother has had him living with her since he started getting into trouble as his grandmother said she could no longer control him. He dropped out of school when he joined the UDF and as a result has had very little formal education. His mother now admits that she is unable to cope with him, either. She is very fearful about his future and is afraid he will die young.

Lucky's case illustrates an ever-increasing problem in the townships – that of children dropping out of school and becoming politicised because of the lack of protection, the poor educational system, the lack of hope for the future. Many become involved in criminal activities and these discredit the political comrades who want to fight for justice.

Lucky's prognosis is poor. He has not bonded with his mother, he has little education, he is politicised and angry and he is out of control. Voluntary agencies do not have the resources to rehabilitate him and others like him.

The murder of Mary Kubheka

Mary Kubheka had eight children. Her brother was imprisoned for allegedly murdering a member of Inkatha. The family strongly denied that he was involved in the murder, but the whole family was threatened with reprisals. One night Mary woke up to a strong smell of petrol and one of her sons said some men had been seen pouring something round the outside of the house. Mary woke the other children aged 2 to 14 and the family got out. The house was not set alight, but Mary decided to take her family to stay with relatives and friends in Johannesburg.

After an absence of three months, when Mary judged that the situation had improved, she came back home with her children but was promptly threatened again. A welfare agency was unable to find suitable alternative accommodation. As she was reluctant to leave her comfortably furnished house empty for too long, she moved in again. She had asked for police protection and she hoped that her family would be safe.

Two months later Mary was hacked to death in front of her children by a group of young men. Her older sons, aged 14 and 19, were threatened and fled, taking the younger daughters aged two, three and four with them. They went to a room in another township. The agency assisted in the placement of the younger children. The older son then obtained a job and said he would support the younger brother. By this time they were living many miles away from where their mother was murdered, yet in spite of this, one Sunday night the 19-year-old son, too, was murdered. There were no witnesses.

In spite of witnesses' evidence no one has been arrested for Mary murder. They gave the names of the attackers, but as in the case of so many other deaths the police have not acted. The young children are in foster care, the middle children are with relatives who still fe reprisals, the 14-year-old is with his teacher and the oldest child is dead. It was because she had nowhere else to go that Mary, in spite of threats, returned to her home and was killed.

Southern Africa – the region which includes South Africa's beleaguered neighbour states of Mozambique and Namibia – has been a moral battleground for humanitarian agencies. Many o their staff on the ground have been outraged by the policies and powers responsible for maimed, disturbed, imprisoned, lost and hungry children, sometimes called 'victims of apartheid'. An aid agency like SCF is not entirely restricted in this situation to relief and rehabilitation. It can and does also make representations to governments and to UN agencies, report to its own staff and supporters, and above all communicate to a wider public what it believes to be illegal or an offence to humanity.

Apartheid constitutes a special challenge to all those concerned bring it to an end. Yet in its effects it belongs to a much wider situation of conflict in Africa. A much greater effort is needed by governments, the UN agencies and the Red Cross to protect the rights of children who are caught up in this conflict. All too often, small voluntary agencies have been forced into the front line of w. to provide services to endangered children. The agencies themselv are inadequately protected and are in too vulnerable a position to help children.

Finally, conflict is impoverishing. The cost of war hampers development and prosperity. Many countries in Africa have defer budgets which take up over 40 per cent of the GNP and there is li likelihood, in the short term, of more investment in agriculture ar education. This leads to a greater dependence on overseas aid and concomitant neglect of children's welfare. The long-term consequence of this is disastrous for the well-being of a nation an its future generations.

Sudan – Hilat Kusha, flooded, August 1988

Somalia – Tugwajalle refugee camp

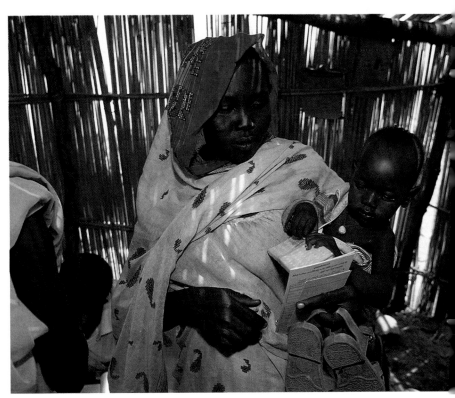

Sudan – Hilat Kusha makeshift hosp..

Somalia – delousing in Tugw...

Ethiopia – Korem camp

*Ethiopia – relief distribution,
Kombolcha transit camp*

Ethiopia – reception cen...

Uganda – camp for displaced families, Lira, 1

iopia – competition for water

Zimbabwe – washing at Binga well

Ethiopia – health education cl

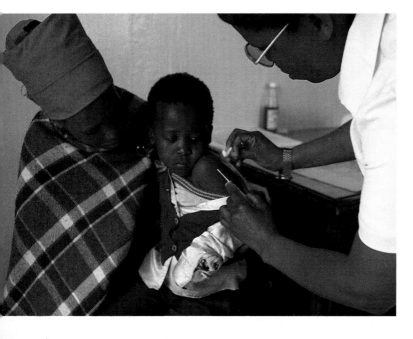

*Lesotho – immunisation,
Loretto clinic, Maseru*

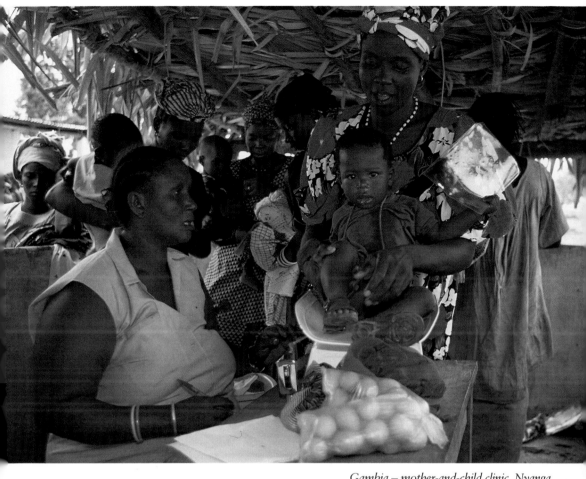

Gambia – mother-and-child clinic, Nyanga

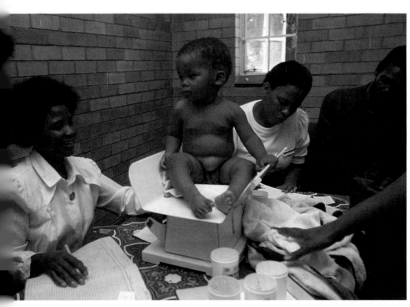

South Africa – weighing-in, Alexandra clinic

Sudan – midwife visiting pharmacy, Woh'da

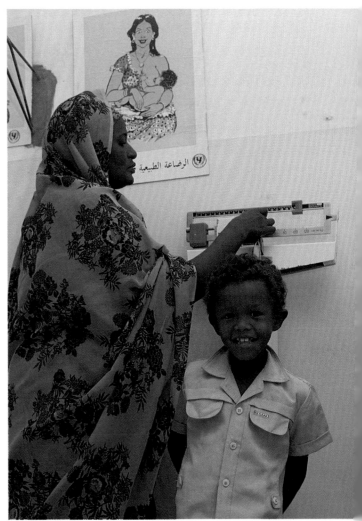

Sudan – clinic, Khartoum north

AFRICAN
EMERGENCIES

African emergencies

Ethiopia – airlift to Wollo

To the western public in the mid 1980s it sometimes seemed if Africa was no more than the sum of its emergencies. Dramatic disasters certainly occur from time to time in Africa; the famine in Ethiopia alone probably took a million lives. Even today there are over four million refugees in the continent and many more displaced in their own countries.

Yet major disasters in Africa are comparatively rare. Africa is prone to earthquakes, and where these do occur – chiefly in the Horn of Africa – with rare exceptions they cause few casualties because of the simple methods of building construction. Great cyclones, storm surges and tidal waves, which in south Asia and Pacific cause death by the thousand, do not occur. Severe flooding rare and relatively local in its impact. The 1988 Khartoum floods were the first to affect the city since the late 1940s.

But by other standards, emergencies in Africa are common. They are often the product of the three linked problems of war, famine and disease.

The effects of war in Africa are devastating, not only through violence but through the disruption of the rural economy and the huge cost of weapons, which can reduce poor countries to bankruptcy. Conflict in Africa, as we have seen, has caused starvation and the mass migration of affected populations; where has coincided with additional problems such as drought, disrupt and death have followed on a vast scale. Unlike sudden 'natural' disasters, economic disasters have deep origins and profound and prolonged effects on people.

For relief and development agencies, the public perception of the nature of disaster is fundamental. The actions of many non-government agencies are inevitably conditioned by the views of the donor public: and it the case of some of the larger international agencies it may be argued that the perceptions of the western public rather than the needs of emergency-affected populations, has influenced the way disaster relief is organised.

In the words of SCF's overseas supplies officer: 'People who want to help cannot easily project themselves or visualise a situation where there are no crops or where they may be seeing their own family or animals die. Generosity doesn't always extend to understanding what it is actually like for people in Africa.'

For example, it is widely believed that famine in Africa mainly arises from food shortages: because of drought or pests, crops do not grow, families are short of food and in the absence of outside assistance starvation ensues. It seems logical that extended period of drought among subsistence farming communities must cause food shortage and starvation. But there is much evidence to conflict with this view. Over the past two decades, drought in Africa has been common. Even ignoring the periods of acute drought in the Sahel in 1968–73, in the late 1970s and again in the mid 1980s, there have been few regular years. Yet contrary to expectations, famine in the sense of mass starvation has been rare. Over the same period it has occurred on perhaps half a dozen occasions: in Ethiopia twice, the second time on a horrific scale; in pockets of Mauretania and Niger in the Sahel in 1972–73 and associated with warfare in Sudan, Mozambique and Angola.

The reasons for this are far from academic. Current systems of relief are based on the assumption that there is an absolute shortage of food and that the response should automatically be the provision of food aid from western agricultural surpluses. This approach has been far from completely successful in preventing starvation. Large emergency food aid operations in remote regions are unavoidably slow. A typical period from the recognition of a problem to large scale action is six months. Starvation has often claimed many lives before food aid has arrived.

Ethiopia – supplementary food distribution

The distribution of emergency food aid has undoubtedly saved lives in specific locations. In Ethiopia in 1984–85, very large numbers were saved by international generosity, and many more who had no food or seed to plant survived on aid during the ensuing years.

But the practical dilemma remains. Although most African food emergencies have occurred after a drought, droughts have not often caused food emergencies. While production failure is now relatively easy to monitor through the UN Food and Agriculture Organisation in Rome, starvation has remained very difficult to predict.

...hiopia – nutritional surveillance programme, Wollo

The issue is, therefore, how do people already manage to survive protracted periods of drought? The explanation is that even poor African communities, particularly in the more risky semi-arid zones, are able to preserve surplus production in good years and can build up stocks of cattle and goods to act as capital which can be realised as food in hard times. They also have an impressive capacity to generate additional food from various sources in times of shortage.

The prediction of impending famine requires not just the recognition of crop failure, but also an understanding of the rural economy. For the farmer the problem of drought may not be a lack of resources as such, but the fact that at times of crisis cattle and other property fall in value and the cost of food rises. It may be possible, therefore, for governments and aid agencies to use food aid more efficiently, both through the market and through distributions, allowing farmers to preserve rather than sell their cattle and other property, essential to long-term survival and security.

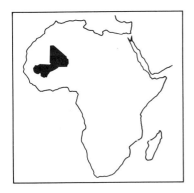

Mali

A year in the life of the Coulibalys

Susanna Davies, an economist with the Institute of Development Studies, and Mamadou Karambe, an SCF Field Officer, have drawn this story from their work on a food monitoring and information project. The project has been investigating the causes of hunger and seasonal changes in the inner Niger river delta and the surrounding drylands.

Samba Coulibaly grows millet in the village of Tomora, where he lives with his wife **Fanta**, three small children and his nephew **Demba**. The family lives in constant uncertainty about where the year's food supply will come from. Their story shows how many subsistence farmers have to struggle to find enough food to eat ever year, not just in years of famine. The year described is poor to fair, following two equally tight years, and is by no means a crisis year.

A major problem for Samba is that all his children are young. He wants to have as many children as possible to ensure that enough children survive and that, as he gets older, enough food will be produced. The area has one of the highest rates of infant mortality in the world.

As there is less than 300 mm of rain each year in Tomora, only millet is cultivated. Samba had to sell his oxen during the 1984–85 drought, so he now cultivates by hand with a hoe. If the rains are good, his two small fields – all that he and Demba can manage between them – will yield enough food for six months; if they are only fair, this will fall to four months. Last year he had to sell his remaining two goats to bridge the gap before the harvest.

In November, after the harvest, the family has to move and split up to find other sources of food, or money to buy it. Fanta will go her cousins on the Niger flood plains to help them with threshing tl rice harvest. By January she will have earned two sacks of paddy, equal to 96 kg of rice – enough to feed the family for an extra month. Meanwhile she and two children will have been properly fed, which is important because she is pregnant as well as breast-feeding the youngest child.

Fanta arranges to meet Samba in the market town of Toguere Koumbe. On the way she picks water lily tubers for her eldest chile to sell in the market. She herself plaits women's hair in Toguere, earning enough to buy another 10 kg of rice each week. But in fact Fanta needs the money to help pay the family tax bill.

Meanwhile Samba has been off to harvest rice in another village and returns to Toguere in February with another three and a half sacks of paddy (168 kg of rice). He then manages to find a few day work brick-making and collecting cow dung used for smoking fish This money is used to buy extra items such as dried onions, salt an perhaps a little fish.

Demba has been less lucky: he headed south to find work in market gardens, and has returned with new clothes, but no food o money.

By March the family have to return home to work on their own fields. Their meagre millet stock is exhausted because two relatives have come to stay, too ill to work in the rice harvest. Samba has only five sacks of paddy, or three 80 kg sacks of rice left. He sells the rice husks to local fishermen for bait and sends Demba to market to sell the rice and buy millet. The price of millet has started to rise because of the dry season, but the family now has four sacks of millet, less transport costs. The relatives leave in April, so there will be enough until the end of June. But this still leaves three months before the harvest.

By May the family is down to one meal a day. Everyone is working long hours in the hot season and needs more calories. When Fanta delivers a baby girl in June, Samba is dismayed to have another daughter, whom he sees as less productive than a son. Fanta's confinement also means that she cannot go out and collect fonio, a wild grain that would normally supplement their depleted millet stock. Demba goes out foraging in the early morning, but this is valuable time spent away from the fields.

But the birth of the child brings good news, too: Samba's younger brother, who left Tomora two years ago to find work in the Ivory Coast, sends a handsome remittance and, with the money left over, they can now afford to buy millet for another few weeks.

By mid August Samba finally runs out of food and has to borrow grain on credit from a local trader. One and a half sacks of millet will see them through until October, but he will have to sell three and a half sacks after the harvest to repay the trader. The interest payment of two sacks equals 160 kg, or enough to feed an adult for a year.

At least the family has come through another year. The rains are reasonable this time, and Samba expects to have enough grain for six months, with possibly a small surplus which he could invest in a goat.

SCF's project, while monitoring the food situation over the whole area, is also trying to identify simple, small-scale projects which will help families like the Coulibalys to improve their 'food security' and ensure that they have enough to eat. Poor families already have a range of ways of coping with food shortages.

Examples of projects include: oxen so that they can cultivate more millet; credit to buy grain during the dry season at lower interest rates; and the purchase of small animals as an insurance against hard times.

Such projects reinforce what people are already doing, rather than impose technical solutions which may not be effective or providing emergency food aid when it is too late to help people to help themselves.

🐜 If all else fails, populations in part or in whole can move in search of employment and food. It is an impressive tribute to the resilience of impoverished rural economies that starvation in Africa has been so rare. In West Africa, millions of people have sometimes been supported entirely or in part from the surplus of coastal economies. In Burkina Faso the income from gold mining, notwithstanding its bad effects, was also a means by which people could support themselves during the 1984 drought.

B **urkina Faso**   *Gold-diggers in Essakane*

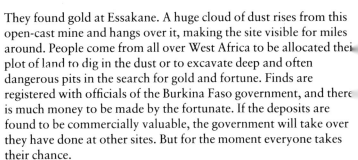

Dr Peter Poore, SCF's Medical Officer, describes a desperate rush to escape poverty in one remote area of Africa.

They found gold at Essakane. A huge cloud of dust rises from this open-cast mine and hangs over it, making the site visible for miles around. People come from all over West Africa to be allocated thei plot of land to dig in the dust or to excavate deep and often dangerous pits in the search for gold and fortune. Finds are registered with officials of the Burkina Faso government, and there is much money to be made by the fortunate. If the deposits are found to be commercially valuable, the government will take over they have done at other sites. But for the moment everyone takes their chance.

There are no government services yet in Essakane, and living conditions are squalid. The abandoned pits are used as latrines. Everything is covered with a fine layer of dust. But where there is money, the businessmen will surely follow.

A regular flow of traffic uses the dirt road approaches to this remote and previously deserted area. The markets are busy and there are many goods for sale.

The miners are mostly men, and come from near and far. They seldom bring their wives or families, and children are not officiall allowed in the camp. The men do not usually stay long, and they a often on their own with money in their pockets.

The prostitutes come from all over West Africa. Their living quarters are the best kept and the most prosperous on the site.

The search for gold which attracts people to this area in the hor of breaking away from the cycle of poverty and disease, may provide the perfect environment for the rapid transmission of the AIDS virus, and its dissemination back to the homes of miners an prostitutes. The virus will be transmitted to their partners and the unborn children, as well as to the prostitutes' future clients. The t of deaths from AIDS will rise.

The last defence of populations attempting to guard themsel from the effects of war or food shortage is flight. The past decade has seen vast population movements, within and across national boundaries. Often such economic migrations are successful: in many situations they terminate in refugee camps, o the slums and shanty towns of the larger cities.

Such emergencies often engage the western media: the wholesa movement of population is a dramatic event. Ten years ago, after the Somali/Ethiopian war, a million refugees moved to Somalia. 1984 and 1985, hundreds of thousands fleeing war and famine

crossed from Tigray and Eritrea in northern Ethiopia to Sudan.
Within Sudan itself, millions have been displaced by war.

Ethiopia

lemayehu and eineba

The reunion

Molla Asnake, SCF's Office Manager in Addis Ababa, tells this story of
famine and migration in Ethiopia and how one family survived tragedy.

It was a bright, clear afternoon. The trees were filled with colour.
Nature seemed to have yielded all her goodness to the environment.

Hussien Taye, resting on the trunk of a tree, examined his
surroundings. He had been living in this village, Adewta Mariam in
Ethiopia's Wollo region, ever since he was born 48 years earlier.
Although he felt tired, he knew that he ought to go back to work.

He wiped the sweat off his brow, and was about to pick up his
hoe when he saw a blue Land Rover coming in his direction. It
stopped in front of his hut. Rubbing the dust off his hands he made
his way towards it. He glanced at the familiar red sign, a child
stretching two hands upward, either for joy or in an appeal to God.
He identified the visitors as a SCF family reunification team whom
he had met, unforgettably, at a place called Sekota four months
earlier.

His first strong memory was of May 1984, when the terrible
drought in Wollo had reached its peak. At that time not only
Hussien's family, but the whole village had suffered appalling
deprivation.

Hope for survival had itself turned out to be a victim of the
famine. Youngsters and adults died or remained weak and
powerless where they stood. Infants passed away at the breasts of
their mothers. By then, every villager would have preferred a silent,
gentle death to a life full of suffering.

It was at this critical time that Hussien, his wife **Zuriash Work**,
his son Alemayehu, 12, and daughter Zeineba, 9, left home and
walked along with other drought victims to Korem. Hussien today
sees it as an escape from life as well as death. Not all were lucky
enough to complete the trip. Zeineba died on the way – Hussien was
carrying her on his back. He and his wife wrapped her in a piece of
cloth, dug the earth with a stick and buried her near the road. With
deep sorrow, he put a marked stone on the grave and paid his last
tribute to her.

After they had reached the camp at Korem, Alemayehu suddenly
disappeared and couldn't be traced. Hussien and his wife carried on
alone, living on dry rations, until the end of December 1985 when
conditions improved and they returned home. On their way back to
the village, they came past Zeineba's grave and wept for both their
lost children.

Hussien said a last prayer to his daughter. 'Zeinu, let God put your soul in heaven. As I know you are innocent, I hope you will hear what I am saying. Since you passed away silently on my back and my own hands placed your body under this earth, your mother and I have been sure that you have gone to your final place, a place where every human being is destined to go. We feel sorry, not for you, but for your brother. We know where you are but we don't know where Alemayehu has gone and our heart aches for him!'

Hussien and Zuriash got back to their village and were gradually able to return to a more normal life. Then one Sunday, while they were having coffee, a group of guests led by the chairman of the peasant association walked into their hut. They brought information about Alemayehu. He had been discovered at the SCF reunification centre in Sekota.

Hussien and Zuriash embraced and fell on the visitors' feet, but were unable to believe what they were told, having mourned their son for such a long time. They now had three days to wait until the appointment to collect him at the centre. It felt like years and years.

Both Hussien and Zuriash thought of the reunification as something more like resurrection, the coming back to life of their child. On the appointed day, when they saw Alemayehu, they could barely control their excitement, but there were forms to fill in – the discharge form, to be signed by the family and someone from the peasant association, the grain ration, and forms for items such as blankets and clothing. After completing the paperwork the couple told the team: 'You have been quite invaluable to us. We cannot pay you back in our lifetime, unless the Almighty does so: human beings cannot carry such a cost. May God bless you!'

By the time of their second visit, the team in the Land Rover were an indelible memory for the family. This time the team interviewed all of them and reviewed the family's situation since the reunion had taken place.

Hussien and Zuriash said: 'May the Lord reward you. Thanks to you, our gloomy life has completely changed.'

Alemayehu said: 'The first week I was home I was worried, I didn't know why exactly, maybe due to the separation from my friends. Later on, I gradually got used to being back with my family and people of my age. My family has a great affection for me and I, too, love them very much. I am also doing well in my class.'

Eventually, the team had to leave. Alemayehu, standing between his parents, waved his hands in farewell. Everyone in the team, too, felt proud of the achievement of the programme. The successful reuniting of a family was an experience for them too, which they would always remember.

The movement of population often presents a serious crisis in its own right. In most camp settings the immediate problem one of health, as people are crammed into crowded camps without adequate site planning, water supply, sanitation or other services. Under such conditions disease often spreads unchecked: epidemics of measles, which may have a mortality of 20 per cent under camp conditions, diarrhoeal disease and other infections run riot. Death rates of 25 per 1000 per day have been recorded sometimes for periods of weeks or months, and total mortality approaching 10 per cent of all refugees in a few weeks have been recorded in some camps.

The refugee emergency of Africa is not just the short-term emergency of relief. Many of Africa's refugees and displaced people have now lived in camps for long periods and represent a chronic emergency of considerable proportions. Somali refugees who were news in 1980 are still in refugee camps. The displaced of Khartoum, who received brief attention and some international relief during the Khartoum floods, are still making a living as best they can.

Sudan

Plight of the displaced

> The example of Sudan shows how, during conflict or in the aftermath of an emergency, humanitarian agencies like SCF can become temporarily involved in a complex traditional society, yet at the same time are recognised as essential in the search for longer-term solutions.
> John Patel, then Field Director, describes the SCF programme there.

Throughout the 1980s Sudan gained a reputation as a sanctuary for refugees fleeing conflict and political strife in the region. But more recently aid agencies have turned their attention to the acute and worsening problems of the displaced people fleeing to the North from civil war in the South.

In early 1988 SCF joined a consortium including Oxfam and Médecins Sans Frontières (Belgium) to meet the needs of a population of displaced people who had congregated in a border zone of South Darfur. Some 20,000 were involved, and significantly the structure of the population was heavily biased towards women, children and the elderly, reflecting the fact that the menfolk had migrated eastwards, driving cattle to new and safer pastures. Thus the displaced of South Darfur had not only lost their traditional grazing lands in the South; their entire system of family life had also been devastated.

The consortium of agencies planned a three-phased programme of assistance based initially on rescue and rehabilitation, followed by resettlement to new sites. The programme has been broadly successful. The key difference between the South Darfur approach and other resettlement schemes is that the target populations are taken to sites where they can establish new and self-reliant lives; they are not taken to camps where dependency syndromes tend to increase.

In the months since March 1988, the problem of the displaced has mushroomed, and in October SCF field teams, working closely with Oxfam, identified groups of displaced people facing appalling conditions, with the worst rate of mortality from starvation ever recorded in the Horn of Africa. In one town they could not even bury their own dead, and many were beyond the help brought by medical teams.

The problem of the displaced in Sudan has now been recognised by both the Government and the international donor community. A UN mission representing the Secretary-General assessed the situation in October 1988 and SCF was included in the consultations and field missions.

Thus SCF is not only providing assistance to large numbers of the displaced, but is also participating in policy discussions where it is recognised as having a key role in finding effective solutions to one of Africa's most intractable problems. The hope is that this partnership of Government, the donor community and non-government organisations (NGOs) will bring sustainable help to Sudan's displaced population.

Hilat Kusha 'place of rubbish'

Chris Thornton visited flood victims in Khartoum in 1988.

Hilat Kusha was one of the districts of Khartoum most badly hit by the floods of August 1988. Even six weeks after the first rains aid workers had to drive their Land Rover along a railway embankment to reach it.

To the left, water covered the road, in places knee deep, spilling over into the streets as far as the eye could see. To the right across twenty-foot-wide ditch, also brimming with water, was the mound known as Hilat Kusha. Translated, it means the 'place of rubbish'.

Situated next to Khartoum's biggest industrial estate this rubbish tip covers about a square mile and is home to over 5000 people, most of them from the black African tribes of southern Sudan. They come to the Arab north seeking refuge from drought and war and looking for jobs. By day they produce goods in the near-by factories, by night, they live among the waste by-products.

Their small one-roomed huts are built with a patchwork of sacking, rush matting, cloth, cardboard, wood and flattened tins and oil drums draped over stick frames. Some of the more unusual looking compounds have hollow car bodies turned on their sides boundary walls.

The rubbish is mainly a mixture of broken glass and tangled bundles of rusting metal. The latter are the remains of metal sheet from which the shapes of cans have been stamped out. There are vehicle parts, discarded bits of animal carcasses and a pile of hoo – presumably from an abbatoir, chemicals, household waste and human excrement.

It is not a healthy place. The smell is powerful, as one would expect. There are flies by the million and rats a plenty. At the time the rains the ditches and pools of water around every hut stagnate for weeks. Effectively open sewers, they formed a perfect breeding site for mosquito larvae and a haven for water-borne diseases.

Hilat Kusha is what is called an 'unplanned area'. Its residents squatters and the Government, chronically short of cash, is unable to provide homes and services for the extra two and a half million people who, like the flood itself, have swamped the capital in the last five years. In September 1988 the Ministry of Social Welfare unveiled a new policy to resettle these people further south in rural areas and make them self-reliant. But that, too, will need massive investment and the Government has appealed to the UN for help.

Meanwhile Hilat Kusha has no water supply, electricity or latrines. The only health care available is a clinic run by the Sudan Council of Churches (SCC). During the floods it was washed away along with a mission school and most people's homes and possessions. As part of the post-flood emergency programme Save the Children helped the SCC to re-establish its clinic, distributed a supplementary food ration to malnourished children and set up an emergency water supply.

The Jelbarra family

Mr Trella Jelbarra, his wife, two girls and six boys, are a Nuba family from Kadugli in Kordofan. They left home five years ago because of drought and travelled to Khartoum by bus. Finding rents very expensive they set up home at Hilat Kusha. Mr Jelbarra works for the council, cleaning, and earns 150 Sudanese pounds (about £10) a month.

Before the flood they were living on the lower, completely flat ground between the mound and the factories but their house was washed away and the lower area became a lake. They had to move up on to the mound which was the area where everyone defecated before.

Mr Jelbarra, a muscular, solidly built man, says it's a difficult life. They eat bread and dried fish and cook one big dish to last the whole day. He says it's not enough but they survive.

His three elder boys, **Mahmoud**, **Jahcoub** and **Yousef**, go to school in the city. Not all the children can go because of the cost of registration, fares, books and school meals. His two daughters, **Jallela** and **Mariam**, help their mother to fetch water – the nearest standpipe being a kilometre away.

The children played football and other games on the lower area until it was flooded. Some children played in the water, however. Rowing in an oil drum cut in half lengthways was a favourite game.

Mr Jelbarra says the children are regularly sick with malaria, eye infections and diarrhoea.

The Mukwuch family

Mr James Mukwuch and his four wives, each with one child, are a Dinka family from Wau in Bahr el Ghazal. They left home because of drought and fighting and came to Khartoum a year ago by lorry. Their journey took 20 days and there was trouble all along the route until they reached Kosti.

One of Mr Mukwuch's brothers is missing. He doesn't know if he's dead, with the Bagarra Arabs who stole his cattle, or elsewhere. Mr Mukwuch earns a living by buying 100 fingers of bread in the city and then selling it in Hilat Kusha. After the flood, bread was scarce for a while and he had to go and queue at 3 am to be sure of getting some. He makes about 15–20 Sudanese pounds a day. Among his overheads is water, for which he pays one pound 25 piastres a jerry can. He uses three jerry cans each day.

Mr Mukwuch doesn't expect to go back to Wau until the fighting and drought are over. 'I am happy I came to Khartoum because I eat.'

 The problems of long-term refugees in Africa are those of refugees in other parts of the world: uncertainty about the future; dependence on aid; the wasting of life. In Africa, especially this is aggravated by a relative lack of international understanding or interest. For the young and educated there has been little chance of resettlement. For the great mass of refugees for whom an eventual return home is the only long-term solution, the levels of international support in food and water supply, education and health services are generally lower than those available elsewhere, and in some cases there would be an international scandal if they occurred in other countries. In some instances food supply has been down to starvation level, and the quality of the supply such that there have been epidemics of anaemia and scurvy.

S omalia

When the solution becomes the problem

David Tolfree made a study for SCF in Somalia in October/November 1987, of a group of some 200 refugee children – ethnic Somalis from Ethiopia – in a large orphanage in Mogadishu. He found that the attempts of outsiders to help had left the children possibly even worse off than if they had remained in refugee camps.

The Somali family, unlike the typically western nuclear family, comprises large family groups which may include grandparents, uncles, aunts and cousins. In the typical household, indoor space basically sleeping space, with communal outdoor areas for cooking eating and day-time use.

From an early age children are exposed to a wide range of social relationships. Older children, aunts and grandparents are likely to share in 'parenting' – it is no coincidence that the Somali term for 'aunt' is 'little mother'. This means the growing child is less individually dependent on one or two parents for care, teaching and control. Great importance is attached to the Koran's emphasis on respect for adult authority. The Somali child therefore has the experience of a more communal form of living.

An essential feature of Somali society is its extensive system of clanship. Although officially discouraged because of its tendency factionalism, clanship gives the Somalis a sense of identity and belonging, and an unswerving loyalty and sense of obligation. This also becomes a form of support to individuals in times of difficulty such as unemployment, sickness, famine or the death of a parent.

When the refugee emergency in Somalia first began in 1979–80 number of relief and welfare agencies began to offer assistance. Among them was a small Canadian-based organisation which was

Refugees in Somalia, 1986

allowed to operate a children's centre in Mogadishu, and from 1981 began to admit from the refugee camps children who were malnourished, ill, disabled or unaccompanied. The centre offered a standard of nutrition, medical care and education considerably superior to what was available in the camps.

What the organisation failed to do, however, was to assess the individual needs of each child or to formulate plans for the future. Nothing was done to maintain and foster the child's family links, and contact with many of the families became tenuous or non-existent. Meanwhile children continued to be admitted with inadequate and often inaccurate documentation. Most serious of all, the effects of separation on the children, including some very young children, were neither understood nor, apparently, noticed. The centre then had to face the consequences of emotional deprivation without enough staff with the necessary skills in child care.

The centre continued to grow, with the government taking responsibility for new admissions of children, most of whom did not even appear to be genuinely needy. To make matters worse, the parent organisation failed to fund or staff the centre adequately. Ultimately it was agreed that the whole operation had reached a crisis point. I was called in as an independent consultant to help evaluate the project and plan for its future.

I began by making a series of visits to some of the refugee camps. The main object was to gain a picture of the child care problems and conditions in the camps from which the children were being referred.

The camps were broadly similar and provided makeshift accommodation, in huts characteristic of nomadic and semi-nomadic people in East Africa. The vast majority of the refugees were women and children, with a small number of older males but few young men. They were supplied with very meagre rations and minimal health care, with some primary education provided by teachers drawn from among the refugees. In some camps there were a few income-generating projects and some organised economic activity such as market stalls. Most of the refugees were obviously suffering hardship and a sense of despair about their future. Families with a lot of children, especially disabled children, faced particular difficulties.

The idea of an orphanage is a complete anachronism in Somali society. The extended family and clanship system effectively absorb the vast majority of social problems stemming from parental illness, death or separation from their children.

While a few of the children in the children's centre were genuinely orphaned, the majority did have parents or other family or community members who could provide care. Admission to the centre offered some immediate relief from poverty and the education provided by the centre was an advantage, but the long-term consequences of losing their links with the community were much under-estimated or ignored.

First impressions of the centre made me very concerned. Although the compound was about 10 acres in size many of the children lived in extremely cramped quarters, with 20 youngsters sleeping in a dormitory about 20 feet square. Sanitary arrangements were very poor, the majority of children defecating in the grounds, with obvious hazards to health. There were no living or playing rooms and virtually no play or leisure facilities apart from a football area. There was an almost total absence of toys, games and personal possessions of any kind. The standard of clothing was low and the food extremely basic.

Staffing levels were poor, few staff had more than a minimal knowledge of child care and there was a notable lack of individual adult–child contact. There was little night time supervision or care. Much of the organising of the centre was left to expatriate volunteers who were, in the main, young, inexperienced and lacking in the necessary skills – though a notable exception was the new volunteer director who had made substantial improvements.

In short, the centre displayed an almost Dickensian image of child care, and I have no doubt that, were such an institution found in a western context, it would have inflicted irreparable emotional damage on its residents.

On the positive side there was a strong sense of community feeling and a remarkable degree of both practical and emotional support towards the younger children on the part of the older ones. There were of course arguments, but these were, in general, resolved in a mature and democratic way at meetings of the whole community. The authority of both staff and of older youngsters was accepted unquestioningly. One of the most startling examples of the care shown by the children towards each other was the use of a curious home-grown sign language which enabled the several deaf children to communicate with others and which led to a high degree of integration of those children.

What the centre achieved – through a process of evolution rather than as a result of conscious planning – was a sense of community quite similar to that which exists in the typical Somali settlement, where a group of families live close together, with shared day-time space which would normally be outdoors.

It seemed that, despite rather than because of the policies and practices of its parent organisation, the centre had drawn on some aspects of Somalia's cultural heritage to create a way of life which, against all the odds, helped to minimise the potentially damaging and depriving effects of institutional living.

Some of the world's most needy children are the victims not only of natural disaster, but of man's bungled efforts to find a solution. The failure of adults to resolve conflicts by peaceful means creates human tragedy on a huge scale. Behind the refugee emergency in Somalia are 800,000 stories of individual hardship and suffering. The 200 children in the centre were also victims of an attempt by a well-meaning, but misguided welfare agency to impose a solution without either understanding the context of the problem, or seeing the potentially devastating effects of their aid on the lives of some of Africa's most vulnerable children.

SUSTAINABLE
HEALTH CARE

Sustainable health care

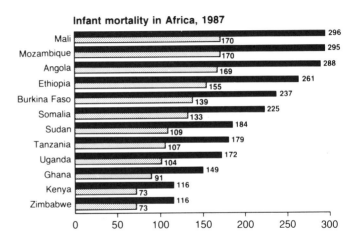

Health is not easy to define. The World Health Organisation (WHO) defines health as a state of complete physical, mental and social well-being, and not merely the absence of disease or illness. Yet when trying to measure health we use such indicators as the average length of life, the numbers of disabled children, or the incidence of disease. These tell us something about the patterns of disease and disability, but they do not tell us about the real causes. Nor do they tell us about the fate of those who do not die and who are not disabled, but who nevertheless may not enjoy 'health' in its fullest sense.

Infant mortality in Africa, 1987

Country	Under 1s	Under 5s
Mali	170	296
Mozambique	170	295
Angola	169	288
Ethiopia	155	261
Burkina Faso	139	237
Somalia	133	225
Sudan	109	184
Tanzania	107	179
Uganda	104	172
Ghana	91	149
Kenya	73	116
Zimbabwe	73	116

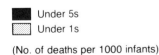

Under 5s
Under 1s

(No. of deaths per 1000 infants)

Source: The State of the World's Children. *UNICEF, 1989*

In the UK we live on average into our seventies, but in many African countries life expectancy is still in the forties. In the UK we expect all of our children to be born healthy and to survive without disability. In many African countries, more than 1 in 10 of all new-born babies die in their first year and up to 1 in 4 die before they are five. Many others will be disabled by disease and/or under-nutrition, especially in poorer communities. There is a consistent relationship between high mortality and poor socio-economic status.

In Africa today, infectious disease is the principal cause of death and disability among young children, made worse by under-nutrition. Today we have several simple technologies at our disposal which can influence the pattern of disease. Vaccinating susceptible infants with potent vaccines can prevent disease, death and disability. Treating children with diarrhoea early, and with adequate replacement of fluid, can prevent death from dehydration (though it does not prevent diarrhoea). We can, then, ease the burden of disease that most young children in developing countries carry, though access to services for the majority of people in rural areas or urban slums is not easy.

Children who survive still have to face the ubiquitous problems of poverty, poor housing, unsafe inadequate water, and the few facilities for waste disposal – either human, domestic or industrial. Food supplies are also commonly inadequate, while education facilities are scarce and often low standard.

Arguably, provision of these basic needs could have a greater impact on disease than the provision of antibiotics and vaccines. The ideal, of course, is to have both, but where resources are limited a careful choice and complementary mix of strategies is necessary.

Poverty perpetuates the problems of inadequate facilities: poor health perpetuates poor health. Under-nourished mothers who are debilitated through frequent episodes of diseases like malaria, anaemia and diarrhoea often give birth to small under-nourished babies which are prone to infection and grow up in a hostile environment.

Improved care and nutrition of children depends on the mother's own state of health and the living conditions of the family. A healthy balanced diet is strongly influenced by the availability of enough of the right kind of food: in the poorest semi-arid regions of Africa, many families are lucky when they can afford, say, a fish or meat sauce to flavour a staple meal such as millet porridge. Malnutrition may also result from unequal distribution or competition for food within the family, and from a lack of awareness or initiative on the part of the parents.

A mother who can read and write will know more about nutrition and hygiene and therefore is more likely to have a healthier child. Provision of educational facilities can therefore have a significant impact on health in the long term. And yet schools are few, books often not available. Sickness keeps children away and there are many other demands on their time at home. Under these circumstances it is unlikely that many will be able to realise their full educational potential.

Women especially bear the brunt of poverty in many cultures. It is they who carry the responsibility for the care of the children and the family. And it is the women who spend most time in the fields producing the food, and then preparing it for the family. Young girls

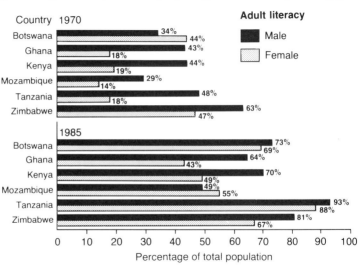

Source: The State of the World's Children. *UNICEF, 1989*

are less likely than boys to receive any formal education. At marriage they are often very young and their child-bearing years take a further toll on their health.

Poorer families are trapped in a vicious circle. Among those who spend most of their time on the basic needs of survival, literacy skill will tend to be lacking. Furthermore fewer people will be available for the posts of teachers, managers, health professionals, politician income generators and other leaders. This in turn can only mean that services suffer from inadequate resources and too few skilled personnel. In all too many cases, the very poor may simply be left to their own devices.

Zimbabwe

Zambezi water

This story by Chris Eldridge, SCF's Field Director in Zimbabwe, makes it clear that health and development in the poorest communities have to start from the bottom upwards. In this example, economic growth and community health both derive from the same source: a reliable water supply.

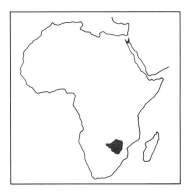

Tazundwa's family

Men rarely fetch water in Africa, or elsewhere in the Third World. This task is performed by women and children, and it often takes several hours a day – equivalent to the time many Europeans spend watching television. Among the most common sources of water, frequently used by both animals and people, are contaminated springs, dirty streams and rivers and unprotected wells.

The spring used by **Tazundwa Mudimba**, living in a small village in west Zimbabwe, is a ten-minute barefoot walk from her hut. It is a muddy hole in the ground with an iron drum sunk into its base from which water is scooped out with a jug. Tazundwa first has to empty the drum, as the water which has collected in it has usually been contaminated by goats, and then she must wait for it to refill. This takes five minutes, and it takes another five minutes to fill her rusty old five-gallon bucket. By the time she returns home, half an hour has passed. She fetches this dirty water twice in the morning and twice in the evening. Two hours of her exhausting day are spent fetching a total of 80 litres – equivalent to two toilet flushes in Britain – for the four people in her family.

Tazundwa's spring probably killed several of her children. She gave birth to 11 babies, but only four survived beyond the age of seven. Her family has always drunk the warm brown water straight – she doesn't know that it contains bacteria. Even if she did, she probably wouldn't boil it because that would mean walking even further every day to collect more wood for her fire.

Much of the sickness in the world, and many deaths, are caused by water-related diseases which mostly kill children. The biggest

killer is diarrhoea, which contributes to 30–50 per cent of the deaths of under-fives.

The combined effect of disease and malnutrition means that in the average African family at least one child dies before the age of five. The bias of government services and aid expenditure towards urban areas means that a second child is more likely to die in a rural family than an urban one.

The difference that a proper well can make is described by **Erica Muleya**, who lives in a village not far from Tazundwa. 'We used to get water from a tank three kilometres away which was filled by water pumped from the Zambezi river,' she says. 'But sometimes the pump broke down, so we had to go to another tank 10 kilometres away. Sometimes that tank was empty too, so then we had to walk for an hour to a dam. The water there had living things in it, and we had to sieve it through our clothes. Now there is a well, so we don't have to walk far, and the water is clean.'

For Erica, as for many rural people, the main advantage of a new well is the increased proximity of water. Several hours of hard work every day can be saved and so women have more time for other activities: growing nutritious vegetables, looking after children, earning money by selling vegetables, baskets, or firewood.

An additional benefit is the improvement in health because of the reduced occurrence of water-related disease. The incidence of diarrhoea drops by an average of 37 per cent when both quality and availability are improved, and when these are combined with better sanitation the reduction is even greater.

Marita Phiri is one of many people for whom improved water supplies in the Zambezi Valley have brought more money as well as better health. After a well was built near her hut she was able to use the increased water supply to grow cabbages, and the closeness of the well means she now has time to sell them in the small town of Siansundu, 60 km away.

Ten years ago the journey would have taken her a day. Now it takes only two hours. In 1986 a tarmac road was laid linking Siansundu to her village, and so she has recently begun to travel there by bus. She only earned £1 on her first trip, but it was worth it. 'I'm coming here again next week,' she says. 'I can't sell cabbages in my own village because there is no one to buy them, but I can here.'

Marita goes to Siansundu because in the last few years the Zimbabwe government has built a high school and a clinic there. Their staff comprise the majority of her customers. She sells her vegetables outside a store built in 1986, after the road had connected the town with Bulawayo, Zimbabwe's second biggest city 400 km away.

Without water to help her grow vegetables, and without the new clinic and school, Marita could not earn her few pounds. Such investment in rural roads, wells, health and education, which only governments can make, sometimes with outside help, have created a modest boom town in west Zimbabwe.

The main benefits of the school and clinic, though, are longer term. If girls as well as boys are given even a basic education – often they aren't because of religious or cultural customs, or because fathers choose to spend their limited incomes on their sons – the

children of the future will gain, as improved maternal literacy is often linked with improved child health.

More rural clinics will also eventually help reduce child mortality, giving women more time to spend on their families' well-being. To raise four children to adulthood, Tazundwa spent many futile years of her life producing another seven babies, years which she could have escaped had she known that her first four children would all grow into healthy adults.

Governments and aid agencies which invest in rural infrastructure are jump-starters for thousands of village engines – people like Marita. Once they are set in motion, they recharge their own batteries. Gradually, more enterprises are attracted to once neglected areas. A private bus service now runs between Siansundu and Bulawayo once a day – two years ago it only ran once a week. A large food company in Bulawayo now finds it profitable to send a mobile grocery store to Siansundu.

These changes in a hitherto neglected, relatively isolated part of Zimbabwe show how small investments aimed at benefiting the poorest people in rural areas can 'trickle up' to other sectors of the economy. But to achieve this the rural poor must be provided with the infrastructure necessary for self-sustaining growth.

Even very basic infrastructure suffices as a start: communal wells – not necessarily individual taps; rural clinics staffed by nurses with basic vaccines and drugs, supported by a network of village health workers with just three months training – not necessarily hospitals staffed by highly educated doctors backed up by electronic equipment; single lane, tarmac or even earth roads – not six-lane motorways.

Villagers are prepared to provide labour and local materials to help supply these services, although some of the cost – for instance, the purchase of cement for school buildings and pumps for wells – will still have to be found from outside.

Home-made wells

The Blair Research Institute of Zimbabwe's Ministry of Health has pioneered the development of several low-cost pumps. These are being installed in rural wells throughout the country under a national water and sanitation programme. Save the Children Fund is supporting this programme in the Zambezi valley, an area which was badly affected by drought in 1982–86. Many rural water supply projects in Africa have failed because the communities they have been intended to serve have not been involved in their planning or implementation. The Zimbabwean government's approach, therefore, is to involve local people from the start.

Many of the rural water points in Zimbabwe's programme are hand-dug deep wells fitted with hand-pumps. Local government councils decide the approximate distribution of water points, and villagers are asked to choose specific sites for wells. Sometimes water-diviners are used to determine the exact location of the well. Villagers build a road to the site and usually contribute labour, sand and stones. The wells are initially dug by hand and then explosives are often used to blast out rock. The wells are lined with concrete to prevent them collapsing, and the pump, which is made in Zimbabwe, is sealed into the top of the well.

The wells, which reach depths of 10–30 metres, take one to three months to complete and serve up to several hundred people. The area around each well is concreted to keep it clean. A drainage ditch, a cattle trough and a basin for washing clothes are often built at the same time and the well is finally fenced off.

After the well has been completed a hand-pump committee, elected by the villagers and consisting mainly of women, maintains and repairs the well's surroundings. One member of the committee is chosen to be the hand-pump caretaker. Caretakers, who are unpaid, are given a simple tool kit by the government to carry out basic maintenance on the pump. They are the first tier of a three-tier pump maintenance system. The second tier consists of 'pump-minders', equipped with a more complete set of tools, who cover several dozen villages every month by bicycle. District maintenance teams, with more sophisticated equipment for completely overhauling rural pumps, make up the third tier.

Other rural water sources in Zimbabwe include dams, and machine- or hand-augered boreholes. Water can be extracted from these sources using electrical, mechanical or wind pumps, and delivered to villages by single stand-pipes or to homes through a network of pipes. The hand-dug well, fitted with a hand-pump, though, has the advantage of maximising community involvement and minimising costs, thereby ensuring that the well will be used and maintained.

B urkina Faso *Womanpower*

Migration in search of work draws many men away from home in West Africa. Mothers often have to fend for themselves and this requires ingenuity. Jumbe Sebunya, SCF Field Director in Ouagadougou, and colleague Marco Weman show how two one-parent families are coping.

The Ouedraogo family

Victorine, Sophie, Regine, Eveline, Sylvie, Roger and **Messan** are all members of a family living in the northern town of Gorom-Gorom – the Ouedraogo family. It is unlike a lot of Burkinabe families in that, with the exception of four-year-old Roger, there are no men living at home.

Victorine is an agricultural extension worker, university-educated, and the head of the household, though reluctant to accept the title. Aged 29, she is married, but since her husband works for an airline company in Dakar, hundreds of miles away, she sees him only twice a year. Victorine takes care of their children, Roger and their baby daughter Messan, besides other younger members of the family.

Victorine follows a civil servant's timetable. She is off to work each morning at 7 am, back at 12.30 for lunch, and then back in the office in the afternoon from 3 to 5.30 pm. When she returns home, she spends time with her children, and, since Messan was born, she has had the twice-daily job of bathing her, especially important during the dusty harmattan.

*Burkina Faso – working mother
at Sebba*

Due to the fact that Victorine is salaried as well as the eldest in her family, she has taken on the extra responsibility of caring for her other relatives and dependants. Her step-sister, Sylvie, aged 17, having failed her school exams, now supplements their income by making porridge and selling it in the village.

Sophie is about the same age as Victorine, though she is actually her aunt by marriage. She has recently learnt how to operate a stand-up loom and the family now also benefits from her sales of finished cloth. When Victorine is at work, Sophie carries Messan on her back while she is weaving.

Regine is Victorine's younger sister, a 15-year-old secondary school student. Victorine gives Regine room and board in exchange for chores – cooking, cleaning, washing, fetching water – which she does around the courtyard after school. Eveline, aged nine, is a relation of Victorine's husband.

At weekends, all the women take part in making and selling 'ndolo', or millet beer, which also helps to increase their income.

Save the Children has been another source of support for the family. They give the children vaccinations and offer the family advice on improved nutrition and health care, with the result that their dependence on doctors and costly prescriptions diminishes, leaving more money for productive activities.

SCF is also providing clean water supplies in the area to serve families at accessible distances from their homes. By reducing the distances walked each day by women such as those in Victorine's family, this allows more time for weaving and cooking at home.

Victorine's children will also benefit from the new public nursery which SCF is organising. Again, this will leave the older members of the family with more free time.

These initiatives are being taken in close co-operation with government departments, and are primarily designed for the benefit of growing children, to ease the burden on families. In the long run, the entire family should become more productive, healthy and happy as a result.

The poorest areas of Burkina Faso are also those areas least suited for agricultural production. When the two months' rainy season is over in early September, there is little to do except wait for the harvest. Dry season gardening has been enthusiastically encouraged by the government, but limited water supplies make it difficult. In any case, productive activities such as gardening are often downstaged by 'quick' money-making schemes like gold mining. The mines have drawn on the supplies of manpower all over the country, frequently leaving homes without the number of helping hands or the cohesion they are accustomed to.

The Diallo family

Fatima Diallo's home, in a village near Gorom-Gorom, is a typical victim. This year Fatima's husband left after the harvest, as he did last year, to mine gold in the village of Essakane. His brother also went off to take cattle to market in the south, and in Togo and the Ivory Coast.

Women like Fatima are seen every day on the roads of Burkina Faso. There are Fatimas carrying faggots on their head. There are Fatimas selling peanuts in front of their houses. There are Fatimas with children on their back, walking through the bush to an unknown destination.

Fatima has five children of her own, three girls and two boys. Also living in the house are one of her brothers and two of her husband's sisters. Managing the household is not easy. Fatima, like many African women, has had to toil long arduous hours to earn what will be considered two decent meals a day for each member of her family.

Fatima used to spend three hours a day searching for water, an intolerable time when she already had to cook, collect firewood, wash, look after the children and relatives, breast-feed the baby, and try to generate income on the side through market gardening or weaving. When SCF repaired a borehole close to Fatima's village it reduced her daily trips by two hours. With this extra time, Fatima bakes dumplings which she sends with one of her children to sell in Gorom-Gorom. This gives Fatima an additional 3000 CFA francs per month (about £5), just enough to buy the textbooks that her son needs in school.

Fatima also has more time to devote to the family's welfare. She takes health care very seriously, always keeping her and her children's vaccination cards up to date, and following up with booster shots. When chatting informally with her friends, though she may not think about it, Fatima is passing on to other mothers vital details about vaccination and nutrition – the most instinctive, sustainable form of grassroots health education.

Fatima's case shows that, once started, development can easily support itself, that people are always capable of improving their own conditions if given some early impetus. Activities as simple as cooking dumplings or baking doughnuts, though seemingly banal, can develop a momentum of their own that affects the community as a whole and improves life for everyone.

Queueing for immunisation

If the family's health is to improve, therefore, and child mortality is to be reduced, primary health care must be complemented by sustainable, low-cost development. A variety of basic techniques have already been developed or adapted in many rural African communities: they include small-scale irrigation, soil and water conservation, stone terracing, and tree-planting. Such techniques can bring in additional family income and provide significant returns, both for the local economy and for the long-term health of the community.

Yet of all the resources available to those concerned with development, the most resilient, adaptable and persistent is the people themselves. Communities usually adapt themselves and/or their environment so as to exploit what is available to their advantage. Giving people the ability to help themselves is more likely to result in sustained development than attempting to impose solutions on an unconvinced and therefore unco-operative community.

It is ironic that this is the very resource that has received little or no attention until recently. The reasons are perhaps not difficult to explain. Politicians, charities, donors and most of the international community want to do something for the poor. But they also need

*Ethiopia – transporting vaccines
by mule, Wollo*

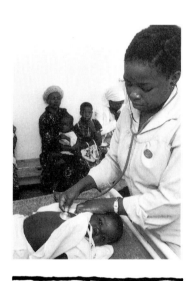

*South Africa – examination,
Alexandra township*

clear evidence of the success of their interventions. This is easy to assess if one simply has to measure the number of children vaccinated, or the number of health centres built. It is less easy if one tries to measure the impact of community participation.

We have vaccines to prevent six of the commonest infections of childhood: measles, pertussis (whooping cough), diphtheria, tetanus, tuberculosis and poliomyelitis. The vaccines are safe, effective, available world wide and relatively cheap. The equipment needed to store vaccines, to transport them and to inject them is also available.

Before 1974 fewer than five per cent of the world's infants were protected against the vaccine-preventable diseases. Today more than 50 per cent have received a third dose of pertussis and tetanus. Much disability and death from all six diseases is being avoided.

The problems of immunisation are not technical. They are lack of management, inaccessibility of the populations at risk, and above all the lack of recurrent funds which will indefinitely ensure protection for all new-born children. But immunisation will require a sustained effort and commitment over many decades from governments, communities, health professionals and from the international donors.

High coverage of vaccination, or oral rehydration packets in the case of diarrhoea prevention, will prevent specific diseases, and they are important. But they will not alone alter the root causes of disease.

With resources scarce and demands great, we must work out strategies which people can afford and which are appropriate for the long-term maintenance of health. These will involve all sectors of government and the private sector, all communities and most important all the people. It will take a long time and will require a sustained change in attitudes.

One of Africa's most serious diseases – one for which there is still no vaccine – is the great epidemic of HIV infection and AIDS now sweeping parts of Central and West Africa. The reasons for the rapid spread of AIDS in Central Africa are not fully understood, though it is clear that this is in part because of the effects of armed conflict and the social breakdown which follows rapid economic change, leading to high levels of sexually-transmitted disease.

The effect of AIDS in parts of some countries in Central Africa is already devastating. Death rates among young adults, the worst affected groups, are very high and there are fears that there will be too little labour available to support their dependants. In one urban area levels of infection with HIV are as high as 30 per cent in some groups, such as young pregnant women, and the toll from AIDS is therefore likely to get worse in future.

U**ganda**

Paulo

Uganda – testing for AIDS, Rubaaga hospital, Kampala

Doctor, do my children have AIDS?

Dr Hanny Friesen, an SCF consultant, specialising in AIDS in children, gives this account of her clinical work in Uganda.

A mother came to our clinic with her one-year-old son, Paulo, because he had been sick for about six months: he wasn't growing (he weighed only 5 kg), had recurrent fevers, and was always coughing. She had consulted many private clinics and doctors and he had been treated for tuberculosis, but despite all these efforts there was no improvement. The mother was healthy, had no complaints, and was expecting her second child.

Because of the history and the findings, we suspected Paulo had AIDS. We discussed it with the mother and we took blood for testing for HIV antibodies. The results were positive.

For some time Paulo did fairly well under our care. He gained some weight, and even started walking.

Paulo's mother duly gave birth to a nice baby girl, who was well for the first few months. Then she became sick on and off with a cough, fever and diarrhoea. One day the father came along to discuss the situation. He asked outright: 'Doctor, do my children have AIDS?'

We explained the problems about diagnosing it in children, encouraging him to care for them as best he could. But his next question was: 'If they have AIDS, is their mother infected?' He finally stopped short before daring to ask: 'Then probably I am infected?' Shortly after this, the little girl died and Paulo a few weeks later. Since then, the mother has produced another baby boy. She is happy, but I am worried.

The transmission of AIDS in Africa has varied from country to country. It has spread rapidly among some communities, while others have remained relatively free from infection. Among age groups, too, there has been uneven distribution. In Uganda, AIDS has been reported in all districts and primarily affects young adults. In the case of children, transmission from mother to baby during pregnancy and/or labour has been the most important route of infection.

AIDS in children can take on the appearance of many ordinary diseases in Africa. Children often show loss of weight, chronic diarrhoea, fever and chronic cough. These are very common complaints, but with an increasing number of women being infected with HIV they may also be the first signs of AIDS in a child. In many cases it is a sick child who is the first in a family to show clinical signs of an HIV infection.

A mother may bring her child to the clinic for treatment of fever or diarrhoea, but the doctor may not suspect HIV infection until later, when it becomes clear that the child doesn't react well to the treatment and is not improving. When the doctor tests the child's blood he may find antibodies against HIV. If a child is below 15 months he may still have maternal antibodies, and in such cases being positive does not mean the baby is infected, but that the mother is and perhaps the father too. To make sure that a baby is infected needs very advanced tests which are not yet available.

Babirye

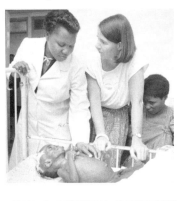

Uganda – Dr Friesen with Dr Mary Nanyongo and 18-month-old AIDS patient, Kampala

In another case, a woman came in with her nine-month-old granddaughter Babirye (a traditional name given to a child who is one of twins). She said that the child was always sick with diarrhoea and fever, that she had seen several doctors but Babirye didn't improve. When asked about the other twin, **Nakato**, and the mother of both children, she said that Nakato had died three weeks earlier after a long illness. The mother, her daughter, was too weak to come to the hospital because of fever, diarrhoea and loss of weight. This left little room for any other diagnosis than 'AIDS in the family', which the grandmother had already suspected. We treated Babirye's symptoms, but couldn't give much hope for a real cure. The grandmother went back home to care for her sick daughter and granddaughter. She never came back, so there was no way of following up this case. Probably the mother and the child have died, and the grandmother is now left alone. Grandmothers often care for their grandchildren after the parents have died, and they have difficulty finding extra money for their food and other expenses, especially school fees.

Education on AIDS

There is an urgent need, especially in countries undergoing conflict, for education on the risks of AIDS among young people. The control of HIV infection depends upon the sexually active population knowing how to avoid it, and behaving accordingly. Providing relevant and acceptable information to those at risk is an essential part of any control programme.

Changing established behaviour among adults is not easy, and knowledge may not necessarily be followed by a change of practice. The education of young children should include information which prepares them for the rewards and risks of developing sexuality and personal relationship so that they are in the best position to adopt a safe and satisfying lifestyle.

Urban health care

The conventional wisdom about contemporary African society suggests that urban populations are privileged groups whose livelihood depends on the exploitation of the rural poor. There is some truth in this, but inevitably the picture is far more complex. The structural reform of many African economies is gradually beginning to alter the economic imbalance between cities and the country. The rural economy is beginning to benefit from higher farm prices and greater investment. Consequently, urban people are paying more for their food.

It has also been generally accepted that rural people have less access to services such as health and education than urban populations do. This view ignores the very sizeable levels of deprivation found within African cities where large groups of the population do not have adequate access to clean water, health care and education.

The population of Mogadishu amounts to one quarter of Somalia's total population. The city of Khartoum has swollen to nearly four million people – nearly 20 per cent of Sudan's population. Sudanese towns like Gedaref and Port Sudan are host to large refugee populations. Nairobi has some of the largest shanty towns in Africa where the municipal authorities are unable to provide sufficient water or electricity.

Populations in the urban slums of many African cities are in no way privileged. Crime rates are higher in these areas and therefore the likelihood of family breakdown is greater. Furthermore infant mortality, because of diarrhoea, malaria, malnutrition and respiratory infections, is often as high in African towns and cities as it is in rural areas.

In the early 1980s, SCF changed its policy and diverted some of its investment from rural health care to providing more services to Africa's urban poor. Today, it has substantial urban health care programmes in Mogadishu, Kampala, Khartoum, Zanzibar Town, Port Sudan and Gedaref. Recently, it has started funding health care projects in some of the black townships in South Africa.

African cities are hosts to a large population of displaced poor. These people often live in 'unregistered areas' of a city, which means that the local government concerned is under no obligation to provide services. These unregistered areas can be huge. In Khartoum, they could amount to about one million people.

The settlement of Al Woh'da in Port Sudan is also an unregistered area which is home to 20,000 Beja nomads who have been forced to give up their traditional life because of drought and desertification in the Red Sea Hills. Home is now a shanty town of packing case wood, polythene, cardboard and flattened out metal cans.

dan – nutrition class, Children's Emergency Hospital, Khartoum

Over the last five years, SCF has embarked on two health programmes in Khartoum and Port Sudan. The latter programme stresses community involvement, and its staff, with the help of the Beja women, have made great progress in improving health care for the children as well as starting up schemes to handle rubbish disposal and latrine construction.

S udan

Acting with the Beja

'The water supply is poor across the whole city, but it is worst in Woh'da,' said Mohammed, a Beja leader in Port Sudan. 'We have little electricity and no sewerage system, and until recently there was no rubbish collection.'

Woh'da, dusty and desolate, crowded with families who had sough refuge from prolonged drought in the Red Sea hills, seemed a good place for SCF to start a health project in 1986. Three years later, with the co-operation of Sudan's Ministry of Health, the project ha begun to influence the whole community through education and training as well as health care.

Sudan – 'the flies' do their dirty work, Port Sudan

'The changes have taken place very slowly because they have challenged people's fundamental practices and attitudes,' says project co-ordinator Jan Cottle. 'It is a good example of small-scal development from the bottom up, with SCF far in the background

One means of getting the message across is the Woh'da mobile youth theatre which delights as well as educates families with animated disease bugs and catchy numbers like the Fly Song:

'I am a weak creature but I do nasty things. In my small legs I carr dirt and germs which make a very healthy person vomit!'

The Khartoum programme, serving a population of about three million people, is considerably more ambitious. It involves improving the drug supplies to 60 clinics and emphasising integrated activities such as health education, immunisation, nutritional rehabilitation, curative health care and midwifery. Great stress is placed on improved management training and on enhancing the skills of key community health workers such as traditional birth attendants. The ultimate aim is to reduce infant mortality, which is very high in the city, and also to ease the burden on institutions such as the Children's Emergency Hospital.

A similar but smaller programme can be found in Mogadishu, where the emphasis is again placed on training mother and child health staff so that a more efficient service can be provided to children within the city.

Very few African countries have an adequate tax collection service, with the result that local authority social services are inevitably short of money and health care within an urban setting is usually chronically under-funded.

Big-organisation donors such as UNICEF can assist with large-scale drug and transport donations, but the weakness in urban health services cannot always be put down to inadequate resources. Insufficient attention to the management of health staff and to correct prescribing procedures also stunts the development of sound health care, and this is where the small-scale intervention of voluntary agencies can be valuable in influencing and changing management attitudes.

Africa's cities have become juggernauts. They show no sign of contraction and the flight from the rural areas because of war or the inability to sustain life on marginal land is increasing the pressure on city populations.

The city places great strain on the African family, often disrupting relationships and dividing family members. All this creates a very precarious, unhealthy environment for urban children to grow up in, leaving them often worse off than the children brought up in villages.

⬛ The health services require considerable recurrent funding for their maintenance. Health professionals must be paid, they must be supplied with essential drugs and equipment. Health facilities need maintenance and repair. Health professionals also need support, supervision and training. This all costs money and time.

Payment for the health services in the long term must come from a variety of sources including the government, the international donor community and the people themselves. Recovery of part of the non-salary costs through user charges is a subject of great interest at the moment. At the same time the costs of the services can be kept to a minimum by the effective and economic use of essential drugs and by adherence to a policy of standard approaches to diagnosis and management.

Drugs which people can afford

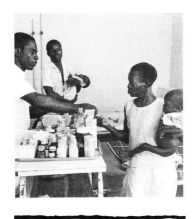

Mozambique – nurse dispensing medicines

Private chemists thrive in developing countries because they meet the demand for medicines which bankrupt national health services cannot provide. Many of their customers are among the poorest in society, which suggests that the poor, despite their poverty, are often prepared to pay for their medicines. John Patel and his colleague Tony D'Souza explain.

For many, the notion that poor people should pay for essential drugs is abhorrent. Their lack of access to a vital component of b primary health care, the provision of free essential drugs, is put down to mismanagement, corruption or donor neglect. However the reality is less sinister; the sheer lack of resources in the majori of developing countries means that comprehensive national healt services cannot be provided 'free'.

Many countries continue to maintain a commitment on paper providing free essential drugs: but there is no merit in such polici the goods cannot be delivered. Unattainable policy objectives actually do harm insofar as they draw attention away from policy initiatives aimed at developing the one resource which will help t poor: their ability to help themselves.

Essential drugs are not a luxury. Over the past 20 years attemp have been made to define a basic list of drugs required for comprehensive primary health care. Low cost generic drugs are n available and in use throughout the world at a very modest unit cost.

SCF has made its own contribution to the process of establishin mechanisms for the secure supply of essential drugs. In establishin essential drug revolving funds in both Africa and Asia, it has donated an initial seed stock of drugs which are provided free or modest cost to consumers at government health centre level. Additional technical assistance is provided in financial managem training in the effective use and prescription of drugs, transport, distribution, storage management and, very important, guarding against foreign exchange shortages. The rest is left to the poor an the revenue generated from their purchase of drugs is used to top the revolving funds.

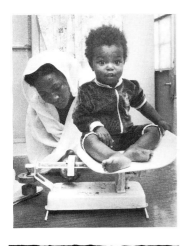

Sudan – TB clinic

An overall pricing structure enables some drugs to be subsidise Thus, life-saving drugs are available free, while others are charge for above unit cost to provide the subsidy. Where drugs are charg for, prices are lower than at private chemists, and also compete w government owned pharmacies.

Lena

Lena Abdul Mageed, aged three, lives with her parents Salwa and Abdul in the Sahafa district of Khartoum. Last year she suffered from malaria and anaemia and was taken to the Samir Health Centre for treatment. Although this government health centre wa adequately staffed with doctors and nurses, there were no basic items of laboratory equipment to help Lena, no reagents to diagn her malaria, or medicines to treat her anaemia. Her parents had n alternative but to go to a private laboratory and pharmacy for diagnosis and treatment.

Alice Akol is a displaced Southerner living in the Shabbia district of Khartoum North. Alice is a chronic asthmatic and requires regular medication to control her asthma. The nearest health centre at Shabbia does not have any anti-asthmatic drugs which she is now compelled to buy from a private pharmacy, if and when they are available, at a price she cannot afford.

Alice and Lena are among thousands of mothers and children in Khartoum who will benefit from the Khartoum Comprehensive Child Health Care Programme (KCCCP), the largest initiative of its kind sponsored by SCF in Africa. The project started at 10 health centres (including those at Samir and Shabbia) in early 1989. Lena and Alice can now purchase low cost medicines at their health centre through a revolving fund established in co-operation with the Government of Sudan's Ministries of Health and Finance and the Khartoum Commission. A range of 70 to 80 essential drugs is available with approximately 20 per cent of drugs free of charge including drugs for emergency care. The cost to the patient is estimated to be one third of what would be paid privately.

The initial response of the public has been very positive, with revenue receipts indicating that the fund should be able to build up satisfactorily. With the removal of many of the administrative and financial hurdles traditionally associated with the supply of drugs through government channels, and by putting the consumers in charge, new sources of funds are coming forward which will mean a genuine increase in the services available.

The principal clients of Khartoum health centres are mothers and children, and the programme makes a direct contribution to improving their welfare. An added bonus is that drugs are more effectively prescribed and controlled, so that the sometimes dangerous influence of poorly trained private pharmacists is reduced.

Mozambique *Nutritional survey outside Quelimane*

During recent years many rural health facilities in Mozambique have been destroyed and health centres that remain open are often stretched to the limit. Generally, conditions are difficult: there is a constant fear of attack, a severe shortage of supplies and a reduced chance of improving the level of health care in the surrounding area.

As soon as an area is declared safe, the activities of health services and agencies are quickly resumed where these exist. Ana Munoz-Munoz describes some of the pioneering work of one health workers' training centre at Quelimane, in the war-torn Zambezia province of Mozambique.

As you fly out of the urban area of Quelimane, the landscape changes completely.

Mozambique – training for health workers, Quelimane

The small plane that is used for those visits (almost none of the roads are safe enough to drive through) lands on a reddish soil that seems burnt by the sun. Almost everything in the village has been destroyed and then rebuilt with dry palm leaves and mud.

It is a long way to the village centre. With no cars disturbing the perfect silence, only the footsteps and the chat of the survey team can be heard. The population has been told to wait around the site where the survey will take place, and everyone knows their role perfectly.

When the team arrives, the community women leaders are rehearsing a welcome song, and nearly two hundred mothers with their children are singing and playing little home-made instruments Greetings, smiles and concentrated eyes are fixed on the survey team, which is ready to work.

The oldest, most curious children are noisy and look at the charts and tapes to be used by the survey team.

It will be a long day, measuring and weighing every under-five child. Most of them will scream, cry or protest. Others, with huge brown eyes, will gaze at the team, understanding nothing.

Cards will be filled in with the children's age, sex, weight and height. There will be extra work later on analysing the data to see how many children are severely malnourished. The information wi be used to provide a logical distribution of food within the emergency programme.

By the end of the survey, everyone will feel happily tired: the student health workers will feel satisfied and useful, and the tutors will have learnt a bit more about those practical problems that nev seem to emerge from the prefab classrooms where they teach.

Health care is a sensitive political issue. Political leaders like to promise free health services. In practice, health services may b free, but they are seldom adequate.

It has been recognised for a long time that government-run healt services in most developing countries are unable to provide consistent and reliable services for the majority of the people.

There are two main reasons for this. The first concerns accessibility. In Africa, the majority of the population live in rural areas. They may live in widely scattered villages with poor or non-existent roads, where communication is limited, and the delivery of any service is extremely difficult.

The second main reason is lack of money. Lack of money for salaries of health staff, for supplies of essential drugs, vaccines and equipment, for maintenance and repair of equipment and vehicles, and for fuel. These 'recurrent' costs are usually considered to be th responsibility of governments, who are unable to fund them from inadequate health budgets.

For health services to be sustained in the long-term, there must b adequate access to a co-operative community, as well as adequate means to pay for the recurrent costs.

The future of sustainable health care services in Africa will depend upon a blend of cost recovery from the consumer, effective management which makes optimal use of available resources, government commitment and international support.

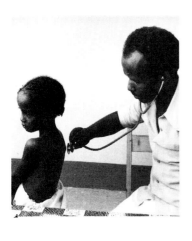

The population of sub-Saharan Africa, estimated at 451 million in 1987, is likely to reach 671 million by 2000 and will have almost trebled by 2025, at 1286 million. Of the 451 million, (345 million excluding Nigera), 203 million are children under 15. The current annual rate of population increase of 3.1% is now beginning to fall and is expected to pass below 2% by 2020.

Source: Sub-Saharan Africa, *World Bank, 1988*

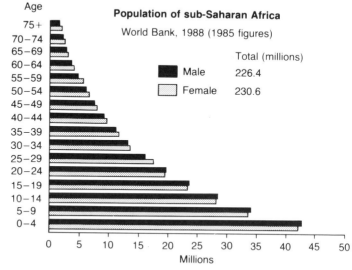

Population of sub-Saharan Africa
World Bank, 1988 (1985 figures)

Total (millions)

| | Male | 226.4 |
| | Female | 230.6 |

thiopia

Zewdie makes a dent in the statistics

Even in remote areas of a very poor war-torn country like Ethiopia there are signs of change, as Dr John Walley reports.

mnesh

Alemnesh, a bright-eyed 18-month-old girl, has been brought to the clinic by her young mother, Zewdie. 'Alemnesh has had diarrhoea for three days,' she says. After examination Belinesh, the health assistant, advises her: 'You should give her extra fluids to stop her getting dry and ill; also more food, so that she won't lose weight.'

The immediate problem is dealt with – but Belinesh doesn't stop there. Alemnesh is weighed and given a measles vaccination. Then Belinesh gives Zewdie a tetanus vaccination, explaining that the injection is to protect her and any future new-born babies. Belinesh then asks, 'Do you want to talk about family planning?' Zewdie replies, 'I don't want another baby yet. I'll take contraceptive pills.' After examination, she is given a packet of pills and told how to take them.

Due to initiatives by SCF, most of the Ministry of Health clinics in Ethiopia's drought-prone Wollo region are now providing a daily mother and child health service.

Not long ago the clinic operated quite differently. Each service was provided on different days. Alemnesh would have got treatment for diarrhoea, but nothing else would have been offered. If Zewdie had requested another service, such as vaccination, she would have been told to come back on another day. Village women like Zewdie often have to walk many kilometres over mountainous terrain to reach such clinics. Zewdie has many other priorities, such as collecting water and firewood. She will come for urgent matters, such as when Alemnesh is sick, but probably not for preventive services.

It is not surprising, then, that less than eight per cent of Ethiopian children are fully vaccinated and only two per cent of women use family planning. Despite the recent famines, the population is growing by 2.9 per cent, and the per capita food production is falling. These factors, together with poor health services, contribute to some of the worst health statistics in the world. Out of every 1000 babies born in Ethiopia, 155 die before they are one year old. Also 20 women die for every 1000 deliveries. These figures are even more depressing when you know that they relate to ordinary, real people, like Zewdie and Alemnesh.

Generally in Ethiopia the numbers of women and children receiving basic services such as vaccination have been falling. However in Wollo, since a daily integrated service has been provided, health care has been improving. Vaccinations, family planning, antc-natal carc, child nutrition monitoring and health education have increased by more than 150 per cent. In many rural clinics these services have started for the first time. Yet there has been no increase in staff or facilities. It has been achieved by helping health workers like Belinesh to work with greater enthusiasm and efficiency.

The Ministry of Health introduced its policy of daily integrated services three years ago. However, the ministry had been unable to implement it due to the difficulties of bringing together the procedures, cards and reporting systems of each of the separate services. Fortunately SCF medical advisers, together with district and regional staff, were able to work through these constraints and establish a model system. Training guidelines were written. Course were conducted at each district health centre, giving clinic staff practical work experience.

SCF have supported, but not taken over, the regional and district staff's responsibilities. In this way their confidence and competence has increased. Because the system does not depend on outsiders, the progress will be more sustainable. What is more, with encouragement from SCF, non-government aid agencies working the region co-operated both in the training courses and in follow-up support.

The Ministry of Health has recently evaluated the Wollo programme and enthusiastically endorsed it. With some modifications they have printed the basic training guidelines and record cards. Senior staff from the capital and other regions are visiting Wollo for practical orientation. Training courses have started or are planned in all regions. Meanwhile in Wollo itself, ways are being explored to extend the support to community health workers and improve health education.

SCF has the advantage over many larger agencies of being able provide long-term, flexible support to health services in developing countries, helping ministries of health to develop better systems of health care. In Ethiopia many more women and children such as Zewdie and Alemnesh will get the preventive health care they need This will help them both to cope with their normal lives, which are often arduous, and to improve their chances of survival when drought and famine recur.

Ethiopia – mother and child, Wollo

THE FAMILY
AS PROTECTOR

*T*he family as protector

In sub-Saharan Africa, the vulnerability of children has been sharpened by the economic decline and recession that have marked most of the past decade. This has been made more appar by the weakening of the extended family system and the lack of a alternative or appropriate support system. From these factors alc stem the bulk of the socio-economic problems that African childi face, both in rural and urban areas. The stories here illustrate sor of these problems, ranging from child migration to towns and th growth of petty crime and homelessness, to the increase in child labour and single-parent families and the difficulties in safeguard children from exploitation and abuse where there are few protec mechanisms.

Rural and urban family households alike are finding it increasingly difficult to look after their own in the current econoi crisis. The economic pressure on African families is three-fold. Household incomes are affected directly by changes in employm and wage levels; falls in agricultural prices further affect rural incomes; and governments, in the face of recession and 'structui adjustment', invest less on social or support services.

There is, furthermore, a multiplier effect on poorer families wl tend to have a larger than average number of children. In times o economic strain, not only do these children get a smaller share o household resources, but some, such as disabled children, may b even more adversely affected within the same household.

*U*ganda

Pressures on family life

Pressures facing families in Uganda may be man-made or the result of natural calamities. They come from war, unfavourable economic situations, cultural and social changes, social stratification, natural disasters and disease epidemics. However, these pressures vary from one family to another. Rosemary Nabatanzi, a Social Worker from SCF's Kampala office, gives examples.

The devastating wars that have taken place since the 1970s have many families without property and lots of women widowed, especially in the war zones. Many jobless single parents struggle bring up their children, usually more than five per family. Under harsh conditions of temporary or inadequate housing, poor slee arrangements and no proper clothing, families struggle to attain life's best out of the little they possess. Trying to replace what wa lost and struggling to educate their children, families who own land are forced to work long hours in the fields. Due to the weakened bonds of the extended family system, individual families have to fight their losing battles alone.

Namigadde's family

Namigadde is a widow. Her husband was killed during the war, in 1985, before he had built any house. The only piece of land he had was taken by his brothers so that the poor widow was left alone with her six children, and no regular income. At that time she was renting a room in the Bwaise slum area and had to pay rent every month. The eldest boy, **Monday**, who was 12, began begging on the streets while the health of poor little **Alex**, aged two and a half, was deteriorating due to malnutrition.

She was in tears when she first approached our office with her six pale children clinging to her. She said she was being evicted from her little room. She asked for help with the eldest two boys because they were turning into delinquents, so they were placed in the boys' home and started going to school. The family had not eaten that day or the previous one, so they were given some posho (maize meal) and beans.

Two days later, Namigadde was back, with her youngest child seriously ill. She had no money for treatment and nowhere to leave the others while she queued for medicine at Mulago hospital. The child was given treatment, but then Namigadde decided to leave, abandoning her two older girls of five and six. The poor souls did not even know the way home.

They were placed in a reception centre and the next day we found Monday and asked him to lead us to their home. On arriving there, the neighbours told us that Namigadde had been evicted the previous day and they did not know where she had settled.

Namigadde reunited with her daughter Annet

About a year later, Namigadde was traced, still as poor and helpless as before. However, she had secured a small plot of land and was trying to put up a house so as to be able to have her children back. She had rented a sewing machine and at weekends had been digging other people's plots to earn money so as to complete her house. SCF helped with iron roofing sheets and nails.

By December 1988 her house was ready and she was reunited with her children. Christmas was a happy one for them. SCF gave Namigadde a sewing machine of her own from which to earn an income, and the children received 'resettlement kits' of household items and tools, and one term's school fees. The older children and their mother have to dig other people's fields in their spare time to earn extra income, but they have all been much happier than when they were in the children's home.

The economic situation facing mothers like Namigadde is heart-breaking. Parents are unable to meet all the pressing needs of children such as feeding, education, health and entertainment. Before one need is met, another problem crops up so that families are forced to make choices. In such a weak and shaky economy, formal education, intended to help individuals to obtain information and skills necessary to live satisfying and capable lives, is beyond the means of most families.

Employment opportunities in Uganda cannot keep up with

population growth or even with the output of school leavers. The lack of opportunities means that heads of families are under severe pressure to meet family needs. Family members become unhappy, and are forced into a situation of apathy. Anxieties accumulate and matters get out of hand, leading to criminality and other social evil such as alcoholism. With its already weakened fabric, the family ca no longer control its members.

Some deprived parents are forced to send their children to beg or the streets or to do odd jobs to earn some pennies and contribute to meals. With poor feeding, the children's health is put under threat and due to the lack of medicine in government hospitals many families who cannot afford private treatment are left to their own devices.

Many families, driven out by lack of housing and high rents, end up in slums or blighted areas of the city to join the weak, the deprived and the demoralised. Families there have to withstand over-crowding, poor health and sanitation, and insecurity. Their self-esteem is lowered by the realisation that they live in an area generally recognised as sub-standard. Their tensions and anxieties are bound to be reflected in activities like crime and prostitution.

Nalongo's family

The story of **Nalongo**'s family is an example. Her eldest son Richa is 11 years old and not attending school. She has twins of about si months, severely malnourished, and a daughter of eight, employee as a housegirl in the city. They all reside in the Kibuli slum area. Nalongo works in an evening market and earns according to how much she has sold. At night, she sells 'waragi', a local beer, from l little room which gets crowded. The 11-year-old takes care of the twins while Nalongo carries out her business. Nalongo is also a prostitute. The children have different fathers but none of them h ever taken responsibility for them. She struggles alone.

Recently, Nalango approached our office, and we gave her a bu fare to her village in Kabale, where she has some land. She can no longer afford city life.

Uganda's cultural and social changes rather than population increase have put pressure on these families. Parents are forced to work all day to earn a living for their families.

Family contact is restricted and the socialisation of young children is put at risk. Family conflicts, the breakdown of relationships and the insecurity of occupations are all pressures which families have to contain.

There was a time when, according to African tradition, large families were highly valued. But having a large family in Uganda nowadays is often punishing rather than rewarding. The extende family system, due to pressures exerted on it, has begun to opera less effectively. The undeniable turmoil which many families are undergoing can only be described as the 'social crisis of our time'

The family is a child's first line of support, and the best chan through which SCF can provide for the child. It is essential t the family unit is protected and maintained. Over time the communal method of rearing children in much of Africa has sometimes worked to the disadvantage of children. For instance, 'apprenticeship' or family labour becomes instead a source of cheap and exploitable labour. The fostering of children can be a disguise for the formation of labour units, and kinship responsibility in teaching a trade may be a purely employer–employee relationship. In Senegal, for example, the system of apprenticeship now provides the hub of unpaid child labour. These changes imply a change in the economic system of production.

African traditions consider children valuable members of society as a whole, as opposed to the family unit alone. Ties with real parents are therefore loose, and children live in a kind of multi-parent community, in which the whole tribe or clan is responsible for them. Education of both girls and boys is provided within a cultural context by different members of society, depending upon the subject taught, and children work in anticipation of their contribution to the community at adulthood. Being a part of the family production chain, therefore, is essential to the child being appreciated.

Yowanina (left) with new family

Yowanina was 10. Her family lived in a village in Luwero district. The day her village came under attack, she ran to hide with neighbours. She heard later that her father had been shot dead as he tried to escape. Their house was set on fire and her mother and brothers were all burned to death. Yowanina found her way to a camp and a woman she knew later became her foster-mother: she called her 'grannie'. She went to Makerere Primary School with the help of an SCF sponsorship. She was 14 when this picture was taken.

Play and the Ugandan child

Despite its troubles, Uganda seems to provide young children with a variety of play opportunities. An unwritten law on play has been passed from child to child, down the generations. Agnes Athieno, a nursery teacher, explains.

In Uganda there is no specific time or place for play. People are always busy with planting, weeding, harvesting, hunting or rearing animals. Work is mostly done manually and no available manpower can be spared. Children of all ages are involved in all types of work, and it is up to the children to fit in their play activities while they work.

While adults are busy in the fields, older children are left to look after their younger brothers and sisters. Children form themselves into peer groups and organise games.

During times of harvesting, children are given the responsibility of keeping birds and monkeys away from the fields. This season is exciting for most children. They compose songs, hit empty tins and make games out of scaring the birds away.

Collecting water and firewood are opportunities for girls to play. Boys play a lot as they go out to look after goats and cattle; wrestling, football, playing flutes and harps are some examples.

All play activities have to be fitted in carefully so as not to offend the adults. The enjoyable game of balancing pots on the head, by girls on their way to or from the well, does not take any extra time. They have a lot of fun turning such tasks into games.

When the wars came, they disrupted all activities, displaced people, orphaned children and left them without security and shelter. Some starved to death. The lucky ones have ended up in orphanages; but how lucky are they? These children have been deprived of many things, including space and the desire to play.

From the start SCF was concerned about the lack of recreation and opportunities for play in Ugandan orphanages. Nsambya Babies Home, caring for about 50 babies and toddlers between the age of one day and seven years, was one orphanage that needed immediate attention. I was employed there as a teacher and nursery nurse. The home was under-staffed and the few workers were kept busy with preparation of meals for the babies, washing and cleaning. There was no time at all for play. The babies amused themselves by crawling around. Babies learned to walk late and with difficulty. Toilet habits were poor as most children could not walk and lacked toilet training.

A play-group was started and after the first year most of the problems had disappeared naturally. Children learned to walk at a much earlier age. They developed an interest in their surroundings and life became more interesting to them.

SCF, with funding provided by the British High Commission in Uganda, has been expanding the play-group into a nursery school that it can also cater for children within the local community.

Franco

Franco is one of the children who has obviously benefited. When the play-group started he was about four years old and was just learning to walk. He walked painfully, with stiff knees and his fingers straight, misery written all over his face. Any slight push could send him falling. I thought at first there was something wrong with him but it was not only Franco. Other children were walking painfully and I found this was simply due to lack of exercise.

I tried out several games with them but most of them were not interested. I had to think of a way of making them play cheerfully and this is the game I came up with.

I got a bunch of ripe yellow bananas and hung it on a post, lined the children up about 50 metres away and explained that anybody who could run and get to the post first would get the bunch of ripe bananas.

The game was played several times. Each time the winner took bunch of ripe bananas and had a rest, giving others a chance to win. In the end everybody got at least one banana.

We repeated this game regularly, using different items such as pancakes, boiled eggs and cassava chips. By the end of the month every child could run as fast as his or her little legs could go and Franco was never anywhere near last.

SCF is trying to restore all the activities that the orphaned and displaced children have been denied. Children are taken out for picnics, to the Zoo, beaches and parks. During the outings the

Mozambique – orphanage

children use a wider environment to play in, swim and generally enjoy themselves.

Games and play activities in the orphanages have to be planned. The children must be individually encouraged, because a sheltered environment does not offer the same opportunities that Ugandan rural children would enjoy under normal circumstances. They cannot just go out and explore. There is no raw material for them to try making their own play things.

SCF has been making efforts to build up these opportunities. Transport is provided and children are taken to rural areas to collect materials for making toys. Banana fibres, for example, are used for making balls, ropes, dolls and toy cars.

A special clay is used for modelling and there is no limit to the toys the children can now make out of clay. Wood off-cuts can easily be obtained from carpenters at very low cost and sometimes free. Rags from tailors give girls the opportunity to make soft toys. These items put together can occupy children for many hours.

Drums and other musical instruments have been given to most of the orphanages. The children themselves have composed songs – songs expressing gratitude to those who they feel deserve it, songs expressing memories of war, and sometimes songs criticising what they are not happy with.

However, life is not all play. While most of these children attend school, they also have to be brought up to become useful and self-reliant citizens. As they grow older, they merge their play activities with simple domestic work.

The same banana fibres that are used for making toys can in different ways be used for weaving mats, table mats and hats. The girls are taught how to sew and weave and they also help in the kitchen and in this way they develop the skills of becoming housewives. There are orphanages that have already brought up children and married them off, thus settling them once again in the community.

Uganda – street children unloading bananas

In rural areas, children begin to work at very young ages, performing various functions within the household or as part of the household enterprise, be it working on the land, looking after livestock, caring for other children in the household, or assisting in household chores such as fetching water. In West Africa there are particular training and communal family labour systems which absorb children in the community at an early age. Young boys will work as apprentices in rural-based, small-scale industries such as blacksmithing. Similarly, young girls take on caring and supportive roles at very young ages.

The economic and social character of the family household define children's well-being, activities, play and value systems as well as the responsibilities of the family toward them. But the African extended family system is now more nebulous and its responsibilities range between traditional and 'modern' approaches. In contemporary Africa, the family role in educating children, for example, has diminished with the introduction of formal education systems, some of whose features are inherited from the colonial period, but which may still include 'traditional cultural' training.

While the plight of street children is intimately connected with the rapid growth of African cities and rural–urban migration, there is no single explanation for the exodus of children to the street. Urban economies increasingly depend on children for widespread use of cheap, sometimes unpaid labour, particularly in irregular, small-scale production and trade. The stories of Kampala's street children may be exceptional, but they explain some of the more general conditions in which such children have to survive, as well as their symptoms, which are to be found elsewhere in Africa.

Those whose home is the street are among the most unprotected of all children. They have little power and no rights to care, shelter, education or health. Some headway has been made in lobbying for children's rights but much more needs to be done on the monitoring and implementation of these rights.

Street children in Uganda

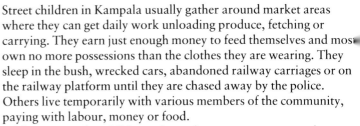

Maggie Brown wrote this article from her experience as an SCF probation officer in Kampala.

Street children in Kampala usually gather around market areas where they can get daily work unloading produce, fetching or carrying. They earn just enough money to feed themselves and most own no more possessions than the clothes they are wearing. They sleep in the bush, wrecked cars, abandoned railway carriages or on the railway platform until they are chased away by the police. Others live temporarily with various members of the community, paying with labour, money or food.

The reasons that children take to the streets are many and various: in Uganda, civil war has divided families. Children who have lost their parents have drifted towards the city. Disease and the effects of poor medical supplies have exposed them to life without adult support. This problem will intensify with the advent of AIDS. Basic poverty is another contributory factor; children are expensive to support and one solution is to allow them to leave home.

A further problem is lack of education. As there are insufficient places in primary schools, education cannot be compulsory. School fees are very high in relation to income and schools insist on full uniform and a complete set of books. Many families cannot even begin to pay fees for all their children. Only 50 to 60 per cent of children attend primary schools and just 15 per cent reach secondary education. For children with no hope of attending school leaving home to work at an urban street market seems rational.

A recent survey of 22 street children, mainly aged 14 to 15 in one area showed that they were almost all from rural areas. Most had dropped out of school because of lack of school fees; some had never been to school. All were boys – most girls in this situation having found employment as housegirls. All but two wanted to stay in Kampala.

The life of children on the streets is dangerous and precarious. They are constantly at risk of arrest by the police who find them a public nuisance. On one occasion, in May 1987, the police rounded up some 40 children and placed them in the remand home, which was overcrowded and short of food for the 60 or more children already placed there.

In the absence of adequate food, beds or staff to follow up their cases, many of the children absconded and returned to the streets.

Around a month later, the police decided to take more drastic action and rounded up 65 children and took them to the adult prison. Security was tight, they could not escape and they faced conditions easily as bad as those in the remand home. They had to cope with the additional factor of being imprisoned with adult offenders. The majority did not appear in court for months, some for as long as a year, and did not know what charges they faced.

There were not enough probation and welfare officers to follow up their cases and they remained in custody. Police were threatening to round up a further 100 children for the same fate and the prison authorities were at a loss to know how to deal with the situation. Such round-ups have continued, some carried out by other bodies such as municipal enforcement offers and the army.

There are other attendant risks of exploitation for children living on the streets. In one extreme case, a few years ago in Uganda, a political party is alleged to have used homeless children as a group of terrorists to rob, pillage and destabilise an opposing faction. The children formed a gang known as the 'Baleebesi' who, as well as leading soldiers to wealthy homes for them to burgle, carried out robberies at gunpoint themselves. The long-term effects on young minds of such behaviour, encouraged by the authorities, must be devastating.

Health is also a constant problem. Many of the children with whom we worked had large open sores which would not heal. They did not have the motivation to queue up for several hours for treatment at the hospital. Sleeping in the bush also has its own dangers.

SCF began working with a group of about 40 children at a market area in Kampala. We attracted the children to come and meet us every Sunday by running football training sessions at a pitch near 'the yard' where they worked. We had a former national football hero who had volunteered to run training sessions with the children and brought along some football shirts and refreshments. A market trader who knew the children individually came along as a volunteer to introduce us to the kids and help to interview them in their own language.

The event proved very popular in the neighbourhood and many other children, mostly from local slum areas, came to join in. In an average week, we had around 80 children playing football.

Initially the children just played football, but they moved on to other sports and activities. As they began to trust us we started detailed interviewing. We wanted to find out how long the children had been living on the streets and why. We also wanted to check out whether the children had any family and whether they would like to contact them. We felt it was possible that some might be able to return home or, if not, could perhaps be helped towards a more promising future in the city.

Michael

Michael, aged 14, had been on the streets for at least two years. He was suffering from a severe ulcer of the foot and limped quite badly. Of all the children he appeared one of the most demoralised and rarely laughed or smiled. He told us that he did not know where his parents lived but that he had a grandfather some 20 miles from Kampala. Michael agreed to visit his grandfather with us although he was clearly nervous about it. On our first visit, he deliberately misdirected us, taking us over appalling mud roads, extending our journey by two hours.

Eventually we met his grandfather. He was a relatively young man who appeared to be in his mid forties and was an elder in the village church. He had a large plot of land, several young children and a thriving business producing local beer. He recognised Michael but had not seen him for over two years and Michael had never lived with him on a regular basis. He told us that Michael's father was a wanderer who had not been stable enough to take responsibility for his son. The mother's whereabouts were unknown. The grandfather offered to let Michael stay with him, but at that stage the boy had not made up his mind what he wanted to do: he needed time to think.

A month or so later, Michael said he wanted to go back and see his grandfather. We helped him to get treatment first and then arranged a second visit. He decided to stay although he was aware that his lifestyle would be completely different. He appeared relaxed and comfortable and several weeks later he had still not returned to the yard.

Livingstone

Some children could not or did not want to return home. One day Livingstone, aged 13, helped us to trace his mother in Masaka, some 80 miles from Kampala. The neighbours told us that it was his mother who had caused dreadful scarring on his hand by scalding him as a punishment. Neither his mother nor father wanted the boy back.

Wilson

Another boy, Wilson, aged 13, exceptionally intelligent and fun-loving, refused to return to his family although they came looking for him. Both these boys wanted us to help with finding them simple and basic shelter from where they could carry on working without the risk of arrest and imprisonment. Eventually they were both found accommodation.

Most of these children are independent and self-reliant. They have to be, to survive. There is a danger that if voluntary organisations provide too much for them in the way of accommodation, food, blankets or clothing and so on, they will become dependent and lose some of their resourcefulness.

In Lusaka, Zambia the 'Mishanga' boys are another remarkably well-organised, if illegal, group of street children who purchase commodities at wholesale prices for their 'retail outlets' on the streets. The boys involved see this as the only means of saving enough to start their own business or of pursuing further education. (See also the case of Nairobi's 'parking boys' on page 98(See also the case of Nairobi's 'parking boys' on page 98

With the breakdown of the family unit, there has been a disintegration of traditional values and cultural heritage. Marriage and inheritance have changed: more women and men marry outside their background and divorced women receive less familial support. Alongside this is the continuing migration to urban centres of family members seeking employment, and the increase in single-parent families running households on one person's income. The vast majority of these single parents are mothers.

South Africa *Maria, 'mother' of 36*

Priscilla McKay describes a remarkable initiative by a young mother in Natal.

Maria Zikhale, herself a mother of two adolescent children, used to work in the hostels in Kwa Dabeka, in Natal. Young women from the rural areas, often in their teens, used to stay in these hostels while they worked in the Frame Cotton Mills. Simple and unsophisticated, living as many as 10 to a room, they often fell victim to the sexual attentions of older men who also live in the hostels, away from their own homes. Maria noticed that these girls, once they became mothers, had to battle to keep their babies with them because the other occupants did not want them there.

Maria left her job and went to university to study for a diploma in community work. As part of her studies she needed to start a project in the community and so decided to start a day and night nursery to provide a facility for the young mothers from the hostels. Initially she took about six children, aged from three months to three years, into her home. Today she has 36 children. A white woman has been helping her and has provided her with two extra rooms with cement floors as her home only has two bedrooms. The babies occupy one room and the toddlers the other. There they eat, sleep and play. Maria does not provide any stimulation for the children but they are fed, clothed and kept clean.

The local social workers are very critical of this service as they feel that Maria is exploiting the parents. However, the children receive better care than they would if their mothers had to send them back to inadequate child minders in the rural areas, where the infant mortality rate is very high.

Maria now needs a larger premises. Money is not a problem as the university has offered to help, but she cannot obtain land to build on because she does not have the backing of the community or the social workers. The township manager is in fact threatening to evict her, her husband and her two children from their home, which formally belongs to the school caretaker and is not meant for running a family business.

This story illustrates the dilemma between meeting a need in the community and providing income for the individual, between social work principles and client needs. The search continues for a piece of land where Maria can provide the service adequately, but the obstacles appear to be insurmountable.

M ozambique *Helping children back into the community*

Bridget Walker gives an account of a vital family tracing and re-integration programme in Mozambique.

Mozambique – orphanage

'You have the right to live in a family. You have the right to a name, so that your parents, brothers and sisters and friends can call you and so that you can be known wherever you are. If you do not have your own family, you have the right to live in a family that loves you like their own child.

'In dangerous situations, you have the right to be among the first to receive help and protection.'

(from the *Declaration of the Rights of the Mozambican Child*, 1979)

In Mozambique the most devastating long-term effect of war on a child is the loss of, or separation from, parents and other family members. If a child suffers these experiences, but later continues to live in the security of the family, despite difficult conditions, he or she is likely to recover more quickly.

In the chaos after an MNR attack, children are often dispersed. They may later be taken in by other families in the community or sent to regional orphanages. In some cases children who are recovered are sent to the capital city, Maputo.

In these cases, in addition to the trauma they have already suffered, the fact that the children continue to live in a state of uncertainty, without knowing whether their parents and family members are alive or dead, impedes their recovery from the trauma. It also means that children are often thought of as orphans, when this may not be the case.

In 1985, a national strategy and policy for the most vulnerable groups of children was worked out in accordance with the Declaration. Those children without the protection of their own family are clearly among the most vulnerable.

Schools, health posts and orphanages are singled out as specific targets for destruction in the war in Mozambique. Thus, in addition to the emotional and sociological advantages of children living with their families in the community, children are also physically safer there.

Three priority groups were identified:

- orphaned and abandoned children in war and drought zones
- street children
- children in institutions

The strategy is to seek and develop effective, low-cost community alternatives for the care of these children. In practice this means first attempting to trace the families, and to reintegrate the children through the family tracing programme. Where this is not possible the work is to encourage and support the traditional practice of accepting unaccompanied children naturally into families in the community, to find substitute families, and to place children for fostering and/or adoption. Increasingly help is being aimed at the whole community rather than individual families, to encourage both integration of the children and self-sufficiency.

SCF are supporting a nationwide family tracing and reintegration programme, co-ordinated by the Social Welfare Department, in collaboration with staff from other government departments and organisations.

This programme started with a course to train trainers, with participants from national and provincial offices of government and aid agencies. During the course, the participants documented and photographed almost 200 children in three centres in Maputo. The methods and interviewing techniques were adapted to take account of the specific cultural and other factors in Mozambique. Posters were made with photographs and other relevant information about the children's families and their areas of origin.

In the first 'pilot' phase, small multi-disciplinary teams of staff who attended the training course worked with local colleagues in two provinces, holding community meetings to explain the project, show the posters and collect further information from family members and others who knew the children. During the initial two days, the families of a total of 31 children out of 40 depicted on the posters were found and identified. The taped voices of the children were played, and photographs of the families were taken, and their voices recorded for the children to see and hear. The emotion displayed at the community meetings as people realised that their lost children were alive and well can be imagined. In several cases it led to spontaneous dancing and singing.

Since then, these and many other children who were thought to be orphans have been able to go home to their families, which in many cases has meant actual parents rather than members of the extended family, and have been settling in remarkably well.

The project has now been extended to six other provinces, and was operating country-wide by the end of 1989. The result is that, so far, over 2100 children have been documented and photographed, and over 500 of these have already been reunited with their families. Now, having seen the results of the work, many other parents who have been separated from their families are joining the project to try and find their children.

Antonieta

Antonieta, aged 12, was living with her family in Homoine district when a violent massacre by MNR guerrillas took place there in July 1987. She witnessed the atrocities of the attack, during which she was separated from her mother. She was subsequently captured by Renamo, and held in the base for nearly a year. She was then freed by Government (Frelimo) troops, and brought to the orphanage in Maputo.

When she arrived, she was malnourished, and severely anaemic. She was completely withdrawn and could not speak or respond, and there were fears that she had been sexually assaulted, and/or had suffered neurological damage, in addition to the psychological trauma, through being hit on the head. After examination the fears of sexual assault proved groundless, but she continued to be mute and respond very little.

After several months, a family appeared in her home province, claiming that they were her relatives, but she was not able to make a positive identification from information and photographs. Finally i was decided to take her on an initial visit partly to see if this was her family, and partly to see how she would react to being in familiar surroundings, hearing her own language (she does not speak Portuguese and this was an added barrier to communication for her), and hopefully meeting people she knew.

When she arrived in the province (by air because it is not safe to travel by road), she stayed in the orphanage while appeals went out on the local radio for her family to come to the provincial capital, from their village. As soon as she arrived in the province she started visibly relaxing, responding, non verbally at first, to staff speaking her language (Matswa), smiling, and after a few days she spoke. One morning an elderly man arrived at the social welfare department saying he was her uncle, and had been delegated by a family meeting to make the quite long and arduous journey from the village to the city, to fetch her home.

A meeting was arranged at the orphanage, and it was immediately obvious from both their reactions that he was in fact her relative – they were both laughing and crying at the same time. The following day she was taken home by social welfare staff, who continued to visit and supervise the family.

It transpired that Antonieta had been mentally handicapped from birth, and had always had difficulty in communicating verbally, but what capacity she had had was blocked completely by her experiences. It was only when she was back in her own area and with her own family that she started to recover.

Antonieta is now living happily with her family, and though they are poor and the area is affected by war, there is no doubt whatever that this was the best solution for her.

For these children, the next phase will be reintegration, when they will be taken back to the areas to live with their families. For other children, the enthusiasm generated has meant that staff are now keen to get the same system going in other areas of the country. Reintegration also involves some material support, as many of the families are displaced and do not have the capacity to support more children. For this reason, SCF is now involved in planning material support not only to individual families, but to whole communities.

The longer-term approach is to help families provide support to children before they reach the point of needing rescue. This requires a structure of normality, such as education and training, to which a family can turn. It also means providing the necessary training to the social and community workers, the health workers, and the educators. At the local level SCF's work in health, education and welfare is largely aimed at helping families to help themselves.

SCF is currently planning with relevant ministries to carry out a more integrated approach to helping children. It is re-examining the roles that institutions can play in the protection of children while exploring the alternative care available in the community. It is also seeking a better understanding of the psychological aspects of helping children who are disabled.

Uganda

Child care services and the law

The laws which governed services to children in Uganda in the early 1960s were similar to those in Britain at that time. Legislation from Britain was passed with few alterations. Uganda was able to afford those services and the rights of children were protected.

Since that time, however, the legislation has not been changed or updated, while in Britain about 40 Acts have been passed. Since 1971 Uganda has experienced economic decline and almost continuous fighting in one part of the country or another. This has led to the near collapse of the system needed to administer children's legislation and child welfare services. SCF social worker Andrew Dunn explains.

Wars and economic decline have created changes in the type of problems facing children in Uganda. The problem of controlling difficult children, which originally led to the Probation and Approved Schools Act, is now relatively minor compared with the rapid increase of children in institutional care, whose number has grown to 2500. In children's homes existing child care laws deal with the problem of controlling children rather than helping and protecting them.

Legislation, even if it is up to date, may not be the most appropriate way to deal with the problems of children in Uganda. In any case the lack of proper legislation is matched by the absence of funds to finance the state social work services. The Probation and Welfare Service is part of the Ministry of Relief and Social Rehabilitation and because of the war it has often suffered from competition for resources with the relief services.

The liberation war of 1979 and the ensuing civil strife (which still persists in northern Uganda) caused large numbers of children to be separated from their parents and relatives, or to be orphaned. The authorities were faced with the problem of what to do with the children. The state-run homes, five remand homes, two approved schools and a reception centre, were unable to cope with such huge numbers of children. The legal mechanisms for dealing with such problems had broken down, courts did not sit and the sudden, vast numbers swamped the system.

The only quick remedy available to social workers at the time was to place the children in voluntarily-run homes, which had been developing gradually since 1979. It seems as if almost any person willing to care for a group of children was enlisted to help.

Information and documentation concerning these children is usually poor or non-existent. The administrators of the homes rarely possess authority from the courts in respect of the children in their care. Fortunately, most of the administrators of the homes are well-intended and care deeply for the children.

It has been estimated that there are probably more than 70 children's homes in the country, most run by voluntary organisations. There is no formal system of registration or recording of children's homes and so it is very difficult to know the exact number. Children's homes vary enormously in style, size and material standards. Homes funded by foreign donors usually reflect an effort to integrate Western values and standards of child care into Ugandan culture (for example, Salem Brotherhood at Mbale). Other homes have been established by the efforts of local and dedicated individuals and organisations (for example, Mama Naava's home at Iganga). These homes rarely have much money and are often overcrowded with few amenities, but children are brought up in a totally Ugandan environment. Another example of a children's home is one in West Nile, near the border with Zaire, where the children live in a collection of grass-thatched mud huts and have no blankets and few clothes.

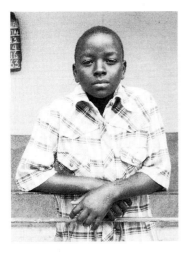

Yosamu Kisa

Yosamu Kisa is an 11-year-old boy from Luwero. His mother died in childbirth, and he and his family escaped from Luwero during the war. His father was later shot and killed, and two younger children died of malnutrition. Yosamu ended up as an orphan in the Nalavule reception centre. Eventually his old home was traced and he was reunited with his 17-year-old brother, John Kusaba. John was given some funds to support his brother, and was then helped train as a tailor at Jinja Polytechnic. Finally, he was able to earn enough to build a new house for them both on the site of their former home.

Unlike some of the State-run homes where there may be more staff than children, most of the voluntary-run homes struggle with very few staff. For example, the administrator of Mama Jane's Home in Jinja manages to care for 50 children with only two staff who work seven days a week for very little pay. At Kiwanga children's home, near Kampala, the staff only receive board and lodging for their labours. Very few staff have received formal training and often left school at primary level. It is very hard for staff to give as much attention to the children as they would have received in the family and in the community.

Currently there are several problems confronting children's

typical day in a children's home

ypical day in a children's ne begins at 6.30 am, about f an hour before dawn. In a wded dormitory the beds are ckly made and the few sessions of the children are ed up. The children go ight to the shambe (field or den) to do the essential work ultivating food crops. The d is either eaten by the dren or sold to buy soap, hes, school books and other ns.

reakfast is usually maize- meal porridge, cooked over an open fire, and served at about 8.00 am. Then the children over six years old go to school; younger children stay until 2.00 pm and the older ones until later in the afternoon.

Education is considered very important by most Ugandans and enormous sacrifices are made by families and children's homes to send children to school. School fees are astronomically high in comparison to most incomes.

Returning from school, the children change from their smart school uniform and either play with balls made from banana fibre or help with chores such as collecting firewood.

Supper is usually maize-meal and beans. Many homes never vary this diet, since alternative foods are too expensive. As it becomes dark at about 7.00 pm and few homes have electricity, the children talk and sing until they go to sleep.

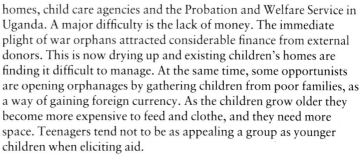

homes, child care agencies and the Probation and Welfare Service in Uganda. A major difficulty is the lack of money. The immediate plight of war orphans attracted considerable finance from external donors. This is now drying up and existing children's homes are finding it difficult to manage. At the same time, some opportunists are opening orphanages by gathering children from poor families, as a way of gaining foreign currency. As the children grow older they become more expensive to feed and clothe, and they need more space. Teenagers tend not to be as appealing a group as younger children when eliciting aid.

The staff of children's homes are becoming increasingly aware that they need training in child care, particularly to enable them to deal sensitively with children who have suffered trauma, such as witnessing the killing of their parents and relatives and the burning of their homes.

There is enormous potential for the development of a child care service which recognises traditional family values as the country develops.

In Ugandan society it is not only the parents who have a duty to care for children, but also the whole of the extended family and clan. During the 1980s a lot of effort has been put into the development of initiatives in the community which help children return to the care of relatives and the extended family. With advice and a small amount of material support most people are willing to take on the responsibility of caring for children of deceased relatives.

SCF is helping to train probation officers to undertake new tasks such as assessing institutional care for children if community care is unavailable. It is also looking at the role of fostering. Generally people are very wary of fostering a child unless the child was abandoned at birth or has no living relatives. The custom of caring for a relative's child dictates that a child can be claimed back from a foster parent no matter what the court has decreed. SCF is also helping to devise training programmes in children's homes and is assisting the older children to leave homes and rejoin the community.

The future of child care in Uganda holds many challenges. A national system of child care records is being drawn up and all the homes are gradually being inspected. In the south a new challenge is being presented by children whose parents have contracted AIDS. This will be a difficult problem to tackle, but at least the knowledge gained in helping children who are victims of war will have been beneficial.

Zanzibar

Help for disabled children

While SCF's Press Officer, Colin Scott discovered this unusual case of disability.

Pascareena

Pascareena is six years old and lives on the island of Zanzibar. When she was three she was struck by a coconut falling from a tree in the yard outside her house. The damage to her brain left her paralysed on one side. She has since had physiotherapy to strengthen her limbs through a unique, community-based rehabilitation scheme organised by local people and supported by SCF.

Every week Pascareena is visited by Mwema, one of five health workers employed by the scheme. She was trained on the island by a local specialist whose own training was paid for by SCF. It is a pilot project which covers just six of the island's villages. Mwema takes Pascareena through a programme of exercises using simple equipment which can be left at her home. At the same time her mother, Maria, learns these exercises so that she can help Pascareena make progress every day.

There are many children in Zanzibar handicapped by cerebral palsy, deafness or diseases like polio. Some like Pascareena also attend a special play-group at near-by Langoni school. Here children who would otherwise be stuck at home and missing out on schooling get a chance to mix and play with others. Meanwhile the parents, too, benefit in a number of ways from meeting each other. Some children get the opportunity to attend their local primary school as a result of the progress they make in the play group.

The whole programme was set up by the chairman of the Zanzibar National Association of the Disabled, Mr K. A. Khalfan who is himself confined to a wheelchair through polio. He wants to expand the scheme to other villages on the island in order to give disabled children the chance they deserve to reach their full potential.

Kenya and Uganda

Disability and family life

African families can provide an ideal environment for the disabled, especially if they are able to play some active part in the community. Chris Saunders, SCF's Disability Officer, gives examples.

There has been a strong tendency in Africa, as elsewhere, to see disability as an illness or medical condition, and rehabilitation as a way of lessening the problem through surgery, therapy, and the supply of equipment. People with disabilities, by definition, have those disabilities for life. In some cases surgery may affect a cure, or equipment may reduce the effect of the impairment causing the disability. This perhaps reinforces the idea that medical intervention is the best course of action. However, doctors can offer little to people with certain types of disability – including those often referred to as 'mentally handicapped', and where doctors do have a role it is a limited one.

Medical intervention, therefore, is usually only part of the solution. Corrective surgery given to a boy whose legs were deformed by polio will probably still leave him with mobility problems. It is probable that he will always have to wear a brace of some sort and do regular exercises at home in order to prevent further deformity. Will his parents encourage him to wear the uncomfortable brace? Will he be encouraged to go to school or find a job? What job prospects are there? The answer to these questions will determine whether the child is successfully rehabilitated into his family and community. The doctors on their own have little influence on these matters.

Two stories from Africa illustrate this question of rehabilitation, especially the role of the family and what can be achieved with relatively little specialist help.

Zanzibar – football game

Mary

When I saw Mary, a little girl from Kibwesi in south-east Kenya, she was about four years old. Born with cerebral palsy, Mary had spent most of her short life lying at the back of her mother's hut on a mat. She was unable to speak, or even to communicate very well. Her limbs were stiff, and she could do little for herself. She still needed help with feeding, and had problems eating solid food.

How can anyone help a child with Mary's special needs living in a very poor Kenyan family, farming a small plot of ground with little time and few resources to spare? In the UK Mary would be provided with a specialised programme involving pre-school placements, physiotherapy, specialist equipment and so on. In Kenya little of this is available. However, Mary's home happens to be in the centre of a project that is developing a range of appropriate facilities for people with disabilities.

The advice given to Mary's parents was to bring her further into

the mainstream of family life. This was made possible by providi
a special chair that enabled her to sit upright and look around. T
chair was made locally and cheaply to a standard design, and loa
to the family until Mary outgrew it. The rehabilitation worker ga
the mother advice on feeding Mary, explained some of the basic
ways of handling and positioning her to ensure correct posture, a
spent time with her family explaining the benefits of attending to
regularly.

As the family began to include Mary in more of their activities,
was inevitable that change would occur. She became more
responsive to attention, which naturally increased the amount of
attention she received. She began to demonstrate in a number of
important ways that she had an understanding of what was going
on. Good eye contact, smiling and general excitement at appropr
times all helped to make her part of the family.

Mary's future is unpredictable but what is certain is that she is
now a part of her family. The chances of her developing to her
potential have been increased enormously as a result of her famil
positive approach.

■ 'The mentally or physically disabled child has the right to a fu
and decent life and should have access to education, training, hea
care, rehabilitation, preparation for employment, and recreation
where possible free of charge. The State shall promote the exchar
of appropriate information about the care and treatment of disab
children. . . . .

From the UN Convention on the Rights of the C

Peter

I met Peter while visiting a project in a rural district outside
Kampala. He is a fine-looking young man of about 15 who lives
with his family on their small farm. He was born deaf, and was
doubly unfortunate when he contracted polio which severely
affected one leg. He has no speech but communicates well throug
gesture. He is active and mobile, using a single pole to help him
move around. He has had no schooling and until recently had no
particular commitment to work, apart from contributing to the
domestic duties of the household.

The rehabilitation worker found there was little that she could
offer Peter in the way of specialist assistance. His hearing disabili
was beyond medical help, but he was a skilled communicator wit
signs, even if his sign system was very much his own. In Europe n
doubt something would have been provided to increase mobility,
but Peter got around well enough and had developed strong arm:
compensate for his inadequate leg.

Perhaps what he lacked most was purpose. He lived in his
parents' compound without any specific role, and with little
prospect for the future. The life mapped out for him was one of
dependence – until what? That is difficult to answer.

The solution proposed was not what one would have expected
from a trained therapist. She did not think of improving mobility
sign language, nor did she try to track down a place in a distant

vocational training unit. Her solution was to call on the skills of the project's agricultural officer, whose job was to work with the small farmers of the area. He decided that pig rearing would be an appropriate activity for Peter, given his restricted mobility and the very small area of available land in the family compound.

Over the months Peter was taught how to construct a pen from locally available materials. He soon collected the materials and built the pen. He was taught the dietary requirements of pigs, again using locally available foodstuffs. He learned the necessary skills to manage first a feeding programme, and then a breeding plan. Each new step was introduced only when the agricultural officer was certain that Peter had mastered the previous stage. At the end of the programme he was sure that Peter would be a competent pig farmer, able to manage a small breeding herd.

What had apparently changed for Peter through this programme was his position and role in the family. He was now taking an active part in the economic life of the community. Although he was not yet contributing any income he was now participating and fully involved. He showed us with pride his small hut in the compound and expressed his hope that he would be able to get married in the near future.

In spite of his disability and the fact that he is living in a relatively poor farming community, Peter has been helped to play a full part in that community, benefit from its training resources and make an increasing contribution to its further development.

)hamed Kizza

SCF's social workers in Uganda have had considerable success in tracing the family members of 'orphans' – children who have already survived remarkable combinations of civil war, poverty and disability.
An arduous search for a blind boy's family finally ends in success – described by the case worker, Fred Kasozi.

Mohamed Kizza lived in Kiwoko, Uganda, with his father, stepmother and brothers and sisters. His mother had divorced a long time earlier and Mohamed did not know where she was. If he had done he would not have seen her for he had been blind in both eyes from infancy. When war disrupted their home life, the rest of the family managed to escape the bombs and the shootings, but Mohamed was left behind because he could not run very far. Some kind people later picked him up and handed him over to the German Emergency Doctors Organisation who were working in Nakaseke Hospital.

A few months later Mohamed was settling down with a group of 30 other unaccompanied children in the care of the doctors when Nakaseke Hospital itself was attacked. The doctors luckily enough managed to escape with all the children to Mulago Hospital where their nutritional state was found to be so appalling that they had to be given special treatment. After six months, the war intensified, and the doctors decided to hand over the children to SCF and the Ministry of Rehabilitation, who were looking after a group of about 150 unaccompanied children at Naluvule, near Luwero. This was where I met Mohamed.

While in Naluvule Mohamed was unable to cope with life because of his blindness. Sometimes relatives or parents used to appear, looking for their lost children; but no one came for Mohamed. I managed to get him out of there, and took him to a foster parent who looked after some children at the Madera School for the Blind in Soroti. We found a place for Mohamed in Madera, but for the six months he spent there he showed no interest at all in learning anything. In fact he tried to starve himself, and then tried to escape, so as to get himself expelled from the school. He refused to talk to anybody, or even play with anyone. He only spoke about three or four words a day. Everybody tried to stimulate him to talk and co-operate with the other blind children, but it was impossible.

He stayed with a couple at the Salvation Army while I got him into another boarding school in Iganga. But he still refused to co-operate. We then decided to remove him from the school and keep him in the hostel while we tried to find his relatives or parents. His mind was totally confused. We even contacted psychiatrists, but without any positive result. Whenever one interviewed him about his family he could say nothing. All methods of stimulating him were tried, but seemed to be fruitless.

Our struggle to inverview over 500 children, scattered all over various children's homes, went on week after week. We had a number of successes, but Mohamed was still a problem. Then one day I interviewed an eight-year-old child called Ismaili in Naluvule. He told me that he had a 'cousin brother' called Mohamed Kizza who was blind but he did not know where exactly they had taken him. I interviewed him further about where they lived and he could not remember, but he told me that they used to run about during the war with 'Maama Katooke'. The chances of finding Maama Katooke now seemed to Ismaili and to me almost impossible. I took Ismaili to the Salvation Army hostel to visit Mohamed who smiled a little when he recognised the voice of his little cousin. I asked Ismaili to stay with him and keep on interviewing him further about their other relatives, but for over two months, Mohamed could not say anything useful to Ismaili.

After some time I realised that 'Maama Katooke' might mean that the children had an auntie or relation living at Katooke, and so had nick-named her 'Maama Katooke'. When we got to the trading centre at Katooke, the people recognised Mohamed, as a blind boy who had hung around there during the war. I became more and more excited. I interviewed more people and one of them took me to meet one of Mohamed's relatives. He could not believe that he was seeing Mohamed again after so many years. Mohamed's response was not the best: he behaved as coldly as ever. They then told me that Mohamed's father had gone to Nabweru, near Kampala, and was working with Uganda Meat Packers, and that his mother had been remarried at Katwe. I was thrilled at this news and thanked the community heartily, before we drove back, planning a further tracing trip around Kampala for another day.

We traced Mohamed's father without much effort. He is about years old, and his joy to see his blind son whom he believed to have died was beyond measure!

He gave us directions to Mohamed's mother's new home. When

we reached her, she burst into tears as soon as she saw Mohamed 'come back to life'. Mohamed's mood on both occasions was an improvement. We took him back to the hostel and his mother promised to contact his father to sort out who would have custody of Mohamed now that they had separated.

Mohamed's attitude to life was changing every day. His vocabulary increased, and he became more and more co-operative. Every other week, one of his parents would come and visit him, bringing something to eat.

Today Mohamed is completely settled. He spends time with his parents in turn and feels quite at home with them. He has been totally rehabilitated, emotionally and psychologically. For me as a case worker, the satisfaction and reward means far more than my monthly pay packet!

U ganda

Young offenders

In the case of many 'young offenders', separation from family has sometimes proved to be the offence itself, as Maggie Brown explains.

Public services in Uganda have been on the point of collapse for some years. The country simply cannot earn enough to support them. What was once one of the most efficient civil service in Africa has crumbled to a point where it is rare in some cases to find a civil servant behind his desk. Salaries are pitifully low, staff have to look for any other means of feeding their families. In the juvenile justice system, qualified probation and welfare officers, graduates of Makerere University earn a monthly salary which is worth the equivalent of just two family meals. Residential staff earn even less.

People continue to work in this field for a variety of reasons. Some were working for this ministry 20 years ago when they earned good money, could afford to buy meat every day, and drive a car. Those people are still shell-shocked and carry on working for the limited sense of security and status the job still offers. Others stay simply because they may get government housing at a peppercorn rent. Others are genuinely motivated to help children and to participate in rebuilding Uganda. Some are tempted to earn a little extra by encouraging parents to place difficult children in care and taking a small monthly remuneration.

In such a complex situation children are inevitably the victims of abuse and neglect.

Not only are the staff poorly motivated to follow up cases of children who have been arrested, abandoned or displaced by war, but they do not have the tools for the job. Transport in particular is at a premium. The only service that seems to have clung on to its vehicles when others were looted is the Prison Department. Thus the situation arises where a child will appear before a magistrate for a relatively minor charge of theft, for example, and there is no transport available to take him to the remand home, so he ends up in the prison.

Together with the Ministry of Rehabilitation we tried to find out how many children were languishing in Ugandan adult prisons, with all the attendant concerns about incarceration with adults. There were no figures. Some staff would try to guess. In Kampala they thought there were only two. Simply looking around the prison compound and dormitories and picking out juvenile faces told us immediately that there were a great deal more. The Prison Department were co-operative; they would like to see these children in a more appropriate environment, but had not managed to keep effective records on admission.

Another major problem is the number of juveniles not convicted of a criminal offence who have nonetheless been sentenced to a three year term in an approved school. Their only 'offence' is being beyond parental control. In general magistrates accept applications by parents at face value, without requiring an in-depth enquiry into family dysfunction. Everyone knows this would not work anyway since the probation and welfare officers have no transport to visit the family. As a result, the child is blamed and incarcerated for three years.

Many of the children in the approved schools (two schools: one for each sex) were fully aware that their treatment had been unjust. They had no recourse to appeal, there was no effective follow up to help to guide them through complex legislation and rules. The Board of Visitors of each institution who would be responsible for hearing complaints and applications for early discharge, had not sat for several years.

Over 85 per cent of boys and nearer 95 per cent of girls in the approved schools had had no criminal convictions.

The approved schools themselves were in a state of chronic disrepair, with no resources for trade training as these had been looted during the wars. Classrooms were, quite literally, completely empty. About half the boys and all the girls went out to the local primary school. The rest were idle.

The Ministry could give the children only posho and beans to eat and sometimes the beans ran out and they were forced to eat the dry dough without sauce. Most of the children slept on sacking on the floor without mattresses or beds. Skin disease spread rapidly, particularly on the frequent occasions when the soap ran out.

The Ministry of Rehabilitation, in recognising these problems, welcomed SCF becoming involved in an overhaul of the system. In August 1987 we began what will probably have been a three year programme.

In the first instance, remand homes and approved schools have undergone some basic renovation to make them more pleasant, healthy and educative places for those children already in the system. Children are getting garden vegetables to vary their diet, and they have been provided with mattresses, beds and tools for trade training.

Meanwhile, we are aiming to bring children as quickly as possible out of prisons into the remand homes.

Staff training sessions are being held to motivate ministry employees to take seriously their role of following up the cases of children in their care.

We are exploring the possibility of using remand home buildings as community trade and basic education centres for the 50 per cent of children never offered the opportunity of attending school. This would allow for a more positive use of the resources already in existence.

Finally, academics, magistrates, judges, probation and welfare officers, solicitors and all involved in the system are being encouraged to consider the direction of juvenile justice in Uganda today, taking more account of Ugandan tradition, so as to build a more relevant system for the future.

L esotho

ebello

The miner's daughter

Marianne Tseng, who wrote this story, is a Danish volunteer working with SCF in Maseru, teaching knitting and other handicrafts at the women's prison.

Tebello is free! She has at last been released from prison after almost two years. She is now 18 years old and ready to start a new life.

When I met her for the first time at Leribe Female Prison, Tebello was a young, very confused girl who cried continually and could not even hold a knitting needle. She had been taken in for stealing.

Tebello came from a remote village in the mountains. She did well at school, but was not able to complete her junior certificate after her father died. He had worked in the mines in South Africa and had been the main breadwinner.

She was the oldest of two girls. Until this event the family had been reasonably well off. Finding it difficult to accept that the family was now poor, she started to steal. Her family say that she became 'crazy'. She was transferred from Leribe to the Female Prison in Maseru, the capital, where all the young offenders are imprisoned. There are approximately 20 to 24 girls between 13 and 19 years of age.

I work at the prison twice a week. There are so many girls there that it is difficult to get to know them all well, so it was a relief when an amnesty was announced and half of them were released. It made it possible to work more effectively with those left behind. Tebello was part of the group who stayed and she made remarkable progress.

Her knitting, until then very poor, began to improve. She was very eager to learn. I realised that she was able to read and write, but more importantly she was able to think creatively. She was soon able to knit difficult patterns. Then the next phase began – she and I made an agreement that she should become my 'counterpart', or co-worker.

I had never been given a counterpart and I always had difficulty in communicating with the younger girls. Tebello, on the other hand, was able to give them the help they needed and the knitting improved tremendously. Together we now make very beautiful mohair sweaters.

Tebello is a sensible girl in whom I have every confidence. She will be helped to continue her education and one day will be able to support herself.

PREPARING
FOR THE FUTURE

Preparing for the future

Uganda – classes as usual

What are the educational prospects for the children of sub-Saharan Africa? African governments are now facing some difficult issues.

The population of Africa is increasing at a faster rate than most other areas of the world, and just under half (45 per cent) is under the age of 15 years. This tremendous growth in the numbers of school-age children places great burdens on welfare facilities which are already under strain from declining economic growth.

Educational provision in sub-Saharan Africa is under scrutiny by governments and aid agencies as part of a reassessment of economic policies and their effects. It is now recognised that some economic policies designed to reduce deficits and pay off debts have disproportionately penalised the poorest groups, especially women and children.

It is generally accepted that a sustained improvement in living standards for the poorest communities will not be possible unless governments invest directly in people by improving their access to education and health.

Education is necessary for development: yet countries at a low level of development cannot afford to pay for it. Some people argue that social services should not expand until a country can afford to sustain them.

What sort of education should Africa's children receive? Should there be greater emphasis on training on vocational training for practical skills, or is this in conflict with the Rights of the Child which emphasise the development of the individual child's personality?

■ 'The child has a right to education. The State shall make primary education free and compulsory and shall encourage the development of secondary and higher education, making education accessible to all and encouraging regular attendance at school. . . .

■ 'The aims of education must include the development of the child's personality and ability, preparation for a responsible life, respect for cultural identity and values, and respect for the natural environment. . . .

■ 'The child has a right to rest and leisure, to engage in play and recreation, and to participate freely in cultural life and the arts. . .'
From the UN Convention on the Rights of the Child

The stories which follow illustrate the complexity of the problem and the diversity of the need. They show the educational achievements of African governments since independence, when many of them started from a very low level in basic literacy, primary school enrolment and further education. But they also indicate that the current economic stagnation or decline has seriously affected the rate of progress in the 1980s.

The proportion of literate adults in Africa's population has steadily increased over the past 15 years, with Botswana and Tanzania almost doubling their rates. But the actual numbers of illiterate adolescents and adults are also growing (though not in Botswana), with 20 per cent more illiterate women than men.

Primary school enrolment throughout sub-Saharan Africa improved substantially throughout the 1970s, with many countries such as Tanzania, Nigeria, Zimbabwe, Mozambique and Botswana achieving universal primary enrolment. But the drop-out rate in some countries is high: in the period 1980–86 only one-third of children in Nigeria and one-quarter in Mozambique actually completed all primary grades. In Tanzania, even though the enrolment rate had dropped to 70 per cent by 1984–86, the completion rate was three-quarters.

Gross enrolment is sometimes shown as more than 100%; this is due to the inclusion of a number of pupils younger or older than the standard age group.
Source: The State of the World's Children, *UNICEF, 1989;* World Development Reports, *World Bank*

Gross primary school enrolment

Country 1960

- Male
- Female

Tanzania
Ghana
Kenya
Zimbabwe

1980

Tanzania
Ghana
Kenya
Zimbabwe

1984/86

Tanzania
Ghana
Kenya
Zimbabwe

0 10 20 30 40 50 60 70 80 90 100 110 120 130 140 150
Percentage

Not only is it difficult to encourage all children to go to primary school, even where schooling is free; it is even harder to ensure that they complete their course of study.

In many countries gains made up by 1979 were lost in the early 1980s. The annual average rate of increase in primary school enrolment at 2.9 per cent is slowing to such an extent that it cannot keep pace with the growth of school-age children at 3.3 per cent.

The pattern of educational development measured by literacy and primary enrolment is uneven across the continent, and although one can generalise (as is the case of Botswana) that the richer the country the better the gain, it is clear that poorer countries such as Tanzania have made great strides forward through deliberate policy choices. But the general slow-down in enrolment reflects the overall economic decline in sub-Saharan Africa, and children who might have gone to school in better times are kept at home to work.

The case for all governments to provide good schooling is strong, irrespective of their countries' levels of development. The correlation between education and increased production and growth was clearly demonstrated in research done in 1988 by the World Bank. The Bank has found that development projects have a greater impact the higher the level of education of those involved.

Lesotho – school kitchen. School fees can be paid in firewood

Where farmers have access to new technologies (for instance, new crop varieties) those who have completed four years' education can increase farm output by 8 per cent. The contribution of an educated work force to economic growth has been measured as high as 31 per cent of gross domestic product.

It has also been proved by UNICEF and other agencies that educated women have fewer and healthier children because educated mothers gain the power to control the number and spacing of their children and pass on a new understanding of nutrition and hygiene through the family. Achieving even basic literacy will give a better return on all investments in development.

Tanzania

Community schools

Tanzania's commitment to make secondary education more widely accessible, and in particular the intention to improve education for girls, shows that even the very poorest countries can achieve remarkable levels of success. Joseph Mungai, who contributes this article, is the former Agriculture Minister of Tanzania, MP for Mufindi District and founder of the Mufindi Education Trust.

> 'When you educate a man,
> You educate an individual,
> But if you educate a woman
> You educate a family.'
>
> Dr Kwegyir Aggrey, Ghanaian scholar and educationalist, 1875–19

In Tanzania during the Nyerere period there was a tremendous achievement in primary education and literacy. We have since enjoyed universal primary education and the highest level of literacy in Africa. In every village in Tanzania there is a primary school. When I went to school in the early fifties the nearest primary school was 46 miles from home and this was common. Today our kids go to school in their own villages, which is a great tribute to the first 2 years of independence.

But primary education alone is not adequate. Parents throughout the country now see the need for a higher level of education. That why a non-State, community secondary school sector sprang up during the 1980s to establish new secondary schools. Today 58 per cent of secondary school children in Tanzania are getting their education in non-State community schools.

Nonetheless, secondary education is reaching less than five per cent of secondary school age children. In my district up until five years ago only 1.6 per cent of children leaving primary schools go places in government secondary schools. The community schools

...nzania – feeding programme at Pwani Mchangani

...anda – Mama Jane's baby home, Jinja

Burkina Faso – women pounding mille

Uganda – resettled family

Mozambique – children's home, Quelimane,1989

Uganda – craft, Naguru remand home

Uganda – art, Naguru remand home

Uganda – street childre.

Lesotho – St Joseph's Secondary School

Uganda – Masuliita Primary School, Luwero

Zimbabwe – boys reading

Mozambique – school dormitory, Minjalene

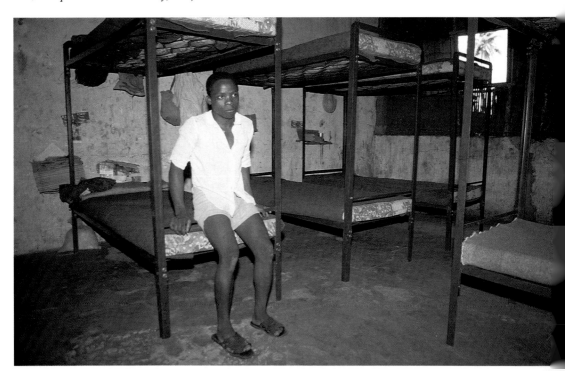

*Mozambique – tidying the classroom,
Escolhina, Maputo*

Africa – Kliptown Montessori school

Mozambique – Escolhina, Maputo

Mozambique – Evening classes, Messica

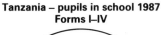

**Tanzania – pupils in school 1987
Forms I–IV**

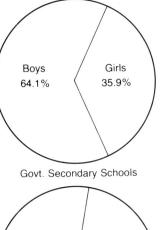

Govt. Secondary Schools

Non-State Community Schools

Forms V–VI

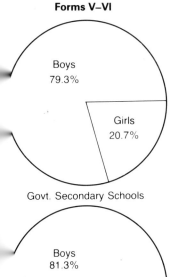

Govt. Secondary Schools

Non-State Community Schools

*Source: Ministry of Education,
Dar es Salaam*

sprang up in response to an emergent need, and by 1987–88 they had managed to boost that progression rate to 13 per cent. The objective now is to achieve a rate of 33.3 per cent by 1992–93.

At independence in 1961 we inherited more secondary boarding schools for boys than for girls. Today girls still trail behind boys in secondary education although the gap is narrowing. In the non-State community schools the proportion of girls has reached nearly 45 per cent within very few years compared to 36 per cent in the long established government secondary schools.

Education for women is crucial in any programme which aims to sustain the level of nutrition of children. Mothers with secondary education tend to have fewer children and these tend to be healthier and better cared for. Education for women is a far more effective birth control strategy than any political campaign or even legislation.

A programme of community schools may be seen as a project primarily to expand secondary education, but it has spill-over benefits for the whole community. By opening secondary schools in carefully selected locations in the rural areas we are reaching more women. The community, not the government, decides what emphasis or bias to give to its education.

In Mufindi we decided our secondary education would have an agricultural bias. We know that not all the children who complete form four will go on to form five for further education, and only a few of them will find urban-based jobs. Having received an education with an agricultural bias and in a village setting they are more likely to opt for a life on the land. During their four years we try to give them adequate agricultural skills, and in form four they take the agricultural exam set by the Ministry of Education. We are very keen to improve the mix between basic education and agricultural skills.

In 1970 when I first became an MP our number one problem was the lack of food and the resulting seasonal migration. Mufindi was then a food deficit district – even for maize, which is the staple food grain. Our soils have over the years been bleached by the highland tropical rains. People went to the warmer lowlands each year to farm, to look for employment, or to buy food.

We solved the problem through the introduction of biologically improved seeds – mainly hybrids – and chemicalisation to replenish the nutrients in the soil. Today we have reached self-sufficiency and surplus. Our people now not only have enough food to eat, but also a marketable surplus which has boosted their incomes. With that income they are able to send their children to the community schools. If we had started the programme of community schools 15 years ago it would not have been as successful as now. It had to be 'food first', and education would follow.

We know there are some parents who still say, 'Oh, we can't pay school fees.' But all we are asking is about 5000 shillings a year (US$40), which is equivalent to five bags of maize. One heifer, sold locally for 20,000 shillings, can pay for all four years of secondary education for one child.

Nobody in our district can say he does not know how to produce 20 bags of maize from one acre, which can easily be managed by one

family even with hand hoes. People can pay fees in cash, or in maize or groundnuts.

Since the 1970s, we have had a strategy of 'Ujamaa' education for self-reliance even at primary school level. We have tried to make the school community a farming community, a community which is learning farming. Teachers should be able to demonstrate modern farming methods, and children should be able to practise them.

This strategy has had a limited success. It has helped us because it is much easier now that we are dealing with farmers who have had primary education. We have raised the production of maize from an average of one ton per hectare to about two tons. We are now trying to go up to four tons, but this is only possible with secondary school sciences – biology, chemistry and physics. Through our community schools we are trying to introduce a new kind of farmer who has been exposed to secondary education and can therefore absorb skill and innovations more easily.

Universal primary education has created an appetite for more education. Education has a new status, no longer competing with the requirements of family labour. Education is accepted as important in its own right and a necessary requirement for the improvement of agriculture, nutrition and health. Families are increasingly allowing their children to go to school instead of working on the land. When the children return home each day they bring new ideas and techniques to the family.

In the 1920s, Mufindi district was the site of the Mumford Experiment at Malangali school. This was an attempt to educate African children in an African environment, artificially created within a boarding school! Today, we are trying to educate children in their own villages, both in the school and in the family, with the involvement of their parents.

α A new emphasis is being placed by international aid agencies and African governments on 'sustainable development with equity'. This means that poorer and disadvantaged people should obtain their fair share of development benefits in a way which can be sustained in the future. Many policies will be aimed at closing the 'social indicator' gaps between countries – for example, by reducing the death rate for children under five or by improving school enrolment. To do this, education budgets will have to be reallocated; during the present economic decline they cannot easily be increased.

Education budgets by African governments vary from country to country. Since 1980 and the onset of economic decline they have been cut in terms of hard cash. Education spending takes up a relatively small proportion of most governments' incomes – a situation which is mirrored in the amount of foreign aid specifically allocated to education; an average of about 10 per cent overall.

There is likely to be a trend away from financing expensive universities – spending on higher education per pupil in Africa is roughly the same as in richer countries – and towards improving quality at a lower level. This will mean more spending on textbooks and teacher training, but probably less on teachers' salaries, which account for about 90 per cent of current spending in primary school

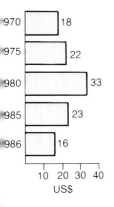

xpenditure per capita

Year	Value
970	18
975	22
980	33
985	23
986	16

10 20 30 40
US$

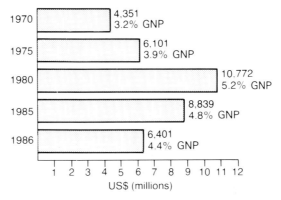

Public expenditure on Education in sub-Saharan Africa

1970	4,351 / 3.2% GNP
1975	6,101 / 3.9% GNP
1980	10,772 / 5.2% GNP
1985	8,839 / 4.8% GNP
1986	6,401 / 4.4% GNP

1 2 3 4 5 6 7 8 9 10 11 12
US$ (millions)

These figures exclude the Arab States, and are deflated by world export prices (1980=100) from International Financial Statistics, IMF, 1988 Yearbook.
Source: Statistical Yearbook 1988, UNESCO

It is now recognised that in the past more aid has gone to higher education than primary, and more has been spent on capital investment, overseas fellowships and technical assistance than on supporting effective national plans. Governments and international planners also now recognise the need to develop education strategies tailor-made to each country's needs, rather than imposing uniform policies across the continent.

Limited cash has forced some governments to seek to recover the costs through fees as in Kenya, or community contributions as in Tanzania. In Ghana, 1989 marked the end of free secondary and tertiary education when plans were published to phase out subsidised meals, books, accommodation and free tuition, with controversial loan and fee-paying schemes. This emphasis on cost-recovery could however lead to a contraction rather than expansion of available education because some people are too poor to be able to afford school fees, however low.

Ghana

Growing up in a mining town

Janet Fishlock describes conditions in Ghana where there is now an attempt to democratise and give more choice to rural areas.

Benedict and Alfred

Benedict is nine years old. He is handsome, bright and creative. The toys he and his seven-year-old brother, Alfred, make from a few used nails and a discarded orange juice can would put western toy companies to shame. There are three other children in the family. One attends a polytechnic in Accra, the other is a mason's apprentice, and the third is a secondary school student. Unlike most Ghanaian families, both parents work full-time. The father, Charles Mensa, is a secondary school teacher, and his wife, Beatrice, is a nanny for a Canadian family at the near-by mine. Together they

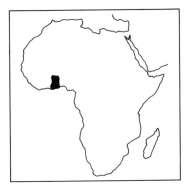

earn US$70 a month – twice the World Bank's 1985 estimate of average family income in Ghana.

The Mensa family lives in Bogoso, a rural town populated by approximately 6000 people, over 300 kms west of Accra. They share two sparsely furnished rooms in a deteriorating cement complex. There is no electricity or running water anywhere in the town. The Mensa children collect wood from the bush to make charcoal for fuel, and they carry water from the near-by river.

Health facilities, education, employment and business opportunities in this area have improved remarkably since the earl 1980s, yet life in Bogoso is still a struggle. Frequent bouts of malaria, tuberculosis, diphtheria, worms and a host of other bacteria-related diseases help to explain that in Ghana life expectancy at birth is a mere 50 years for men and 54 for women.

At the Bogoso health centre, where 19 staff serve villages within an 11 mile radius, they see an average of 500 patients per month. Over 30 per cent are treated for malaria. With no transport, insufficient diagnostic equipment, limited medical supplies, and on large room with four beds, the centre's effectiveness is limited.

The local education system suffers from similar shortages. Benedict and Alfred attend a small private school. According to M Mensa: 'Although the government-run primary schools only char; a small fee, the teachers are poorly paid, there are no textbooks, n paper, no chalk. So they send the children out to collect wood so t school can make some money . . .'.

Even the private schools are ill-equipped and in many cases poorly managed. The school the Mensa children attend is a cemer shelter with thin bamboo dividers for walls. A piece of wood serv as a blackboard – when chalk is available. Goats, chickens, sheep and pigs wander through the school. During the rainy season, students huddle in the classroom shivering until the headmaster decides to close the school for the day. Mrs Mensa was until recei the nursery teacher: 'Our nursery has no toys, just a few straw ma for the children to sit on. Many come to school with fevers and coughs, and we have nothing to give them . . .'.

The lack of resources coupled with low salaries, results in teacl who are frustrated, unmotivated and often lacking any formal training. Alfred's teacher is one: 'When I finished form five I want to go to hairdressing school, but it costs too much. I don't really l teaching, but it gives me some money . . .'.

In the 1984 census, the Ghana government found that 40 per c of the school-age population in the western region had never attended school. Of the primary school teachers, 49 per cent wer considered 'untrained'.

In a country of close to 13 million, there are only three universities with a total enrolment of 9000. Even at that level, resources are scarce. Lecturers are paid an average of US$50 a month. When students heard that the government was consideri charging students for tuition, just prior to the 1988 final exams, went on strike. They demanded an increase in the meagre studen allowance, and condemned the government's plan to institute tuition fees. The strike lasted more than four months.

It's a vicious circle. Many people cannot afford to pay for

education, yet within their present budget, schools cannot survive, let alone improve in quality. And there is increasing demand from new and expanding businesses and industries, particularly those coming in from other countries, for educated and skilled labour.

The mine in Bogoso prefers to hire local people though most lack specific skills and the necessary education. Of nearly 100 Ghanaian employees, less than 10 have more than secondary school education.

In spite of these bleak realities, the future does look positive. The government has taken steps to decentralise and democratise the political process. It is now attempting to encourage people in both rural and urban areas to communicate their needs and concerns. As one headteacher points out: 'The government is finally recognising that the country's wealth is in the rural areas, and that they deserve a voice in what happens in the country.'

The UN Convention on the Rights of the Child obliges governments to 'make education compulsory and available free to all' and secondary education 'available and accessible to every child'. Of 11 countries studied in this chapter, five (Botswana, Kenya, Sierra Leone, Sudan and Uganda) do not have compulsory primary education. In the remaining six, the starting age and duration varies. The legal school leaving age, for example, ranges from 12 in Nigeria to 16 in Ghana.

All training – and teachers' training in particular – needs to be responsive to local conditions. In Africa most children have to bridge a wide gap between home and school because they are often not taught in their mother tongue and are unused to written communication and the routine of formal learning. A teacher's function in enabling a child to acquire new and, at first, alien ideas and skills is absolutely vital and depends upon the right sort of training.

Most sub-Saharan African countries now include some form of vocational training in their curricula, even at primary level. Acquiring practical skills, whether agricultural, mechanical or craft-oriented is seen by many planners as a necessity for development. It is also generally accepted that achieving a good basic education which improves 'cognitive' skills (the raised level of understanding and ability which comes from numeracy and literacy) is the most effective way of producing a trainable work force. Choices at secondary level between continuing general education, and emphasising vocational or specialist skills will depend on each country's particular need. But the idea of designing curricula to produce a work force which will serve the economy more efficiently is seen by some to inhibit personal development and intellectual freedom.

Similarly education which offers up-to-date training and skills will enable Africans to use their own resources to improve standards of living. Most Africans today are eager to learn about modern technology and methods of production. But some are wary of an over-emphasis on training for jobs through a school system which promotes competition and selection. They believe that traditional African values based on community learning and sharing could be promoted better through less formal schooling.

…zambique – primary school in Quelimane. SCF has supplied light fittings and door locks

Education and learning do not, of course, have to be confined to school. It is too expensive to provide enough school buildings and staff close to the communities of about two-thirds of sub-Saharan Africa's people, who are rural and scattered over great distances. Informal teaching which uses radio broadcasts, correspondence courses, community activities and local apprenticeships is often the only way for children in rural areas to learn.

Many of the personal accounts in this chapter describe curricula and programmes designed to improve employment opportunities, but they also show how the acquisition of practical skills is no guarantee of a job. As the level of education rises in Kenya, employers become more demanding and expect higher qualifications from applicants than may actually be necessary.

Kenya

School-leavers head for the sun

Geoffrey Griffin describes the growth of the informal sector in meeting the demand for training and jobs.

In 1964, when Kenya became independent, the shortage of educat youth was such that employers contended for the services of any b or girl who had completed 'O' levels. At that time, the country had only 151 secondary schools, but as a result of massive investment they now number 2400.

As time passed, 'A' level leavers came increasingly to compete for and dominate the work-openings for which 'O' level leavers were previously taken. Faced with the task of selecting from among hundreds of applicants for each opening, employers tend to choos those with the highest educational certificates, even though the jok in question may not require such a level for their successful performance.

In 1983, the Government introduced a new system, known to a as '8:4:4', meaning eight years primary schooling, four years secondary schooling and four years for a general degree. The number of school subjects was increased, with a strong emphasis being placed on agriculture, practical subjects and business education. The first secondary examination for 8:4:4 pupils was held in 1989.

However, it is apparent that population growth and the ever-increasing number of school-leavers must still swamp employmer openings, no matter how the educational ladder is structured. Indeed, the forecast is that, by the year 2000, the demand for facilities for formal education will have doubled, with seven milli pupils in primary schools and one million in secondary schools.

In such a situation there is a natural tendency to look to techni training to provide a happy solution in preparing youth for gainf work. But the same problem soon shows itself. In Kenya, large numbers of youth centres or 'village polytechnics', sponsored by local communities, churches or non-government organisations (NGOs), have provided basic artisan training for a very long time. Their contribution has been invaluable and has helped many individuals to gain a living, but sooner or later the area round about each institution becomes saturated with carpenters, shoe-repairers or whatever other trade is being taught. To remain viable, the institution may be forced to retire its instructors, hire new ones and re-tool for other trades; or else build dormitories and seek to attract trainees from further afield at greater cost.

At craftsman level, there are the big Institutes of Technology, built under Kenya's unique 'Harambee' system of voluntary giving by the public. Graduates from these can seek employment anywhere in the country, but recent studies show that an increasing percentage, particularly in the building trades, are unable to find salaried work. Kenya's uniformed and very efficient National Youth Service provides training at craft or junior technician levels. Its trainees, with the additional attraction of their disciplined background, have been much favoured by employers for over two decades, but nowadays 'ex-servicemen' with excellent certificates are starting to find that the jobs aren't there in some occupations.

So what about the fostering of self-employment through technical skills? The National Youth Service has experimented with training men as village artisans by giving them a range of inter-related skills instead of narrow specialisations, including basic business knowledge in the course and by helping them to obtain loans to set up their own workshops. This scheme has resulted in some fine successes, but it is so time-consuming and costly that the numbers going through it remain small.

Drawing increasing attention is a sector known as 'Jua Kali'. Meaning 'Fierce Sun', it embraces those who, without even shelter under which to work, salvage materials from wherever they can and, showing considerable ingenuity, transform them into cheap saleable articles that are in constant demand – buckets, charcoal stoves, tin trunks, simple furniture and the like: others undertake roadside repairs of anything from wheelbarrows to lorries. President Moi has himself initiated measures to help this sector to organise itself and obtain better working conditions, credit facilities and markets for its products. As a result, some 'Jua Kali' workers are venturing into the production of machines such as maize-grinders, pumps and threshers – to the benefit of Kenya's agricultural base.

The present number of 'Jua Kali' artisans is estimated at 200,000, most of whom acquired their skills through informal apprenticeships and on-the-job training. The sector could well double in size by the turn of the century as it is reinforced by school-leavers who, under the new educational system, have had some exposure to the use of tools.

For NGOs, the lesson is that the days have gone when, in enthusiastic zeal to help the poor boys and girls of some particular locality, a technical training centre could be quickly established to teach simple metalwork, auto-mechanics or dress-making. Kenya still has great need for technical training and investment which is very welcome. But, in designing schemes, it is now a question of careful research, in close liaison with the authorities, to identify areas where skilled labour is lacking. The wise planner will aim to diversify courses as much as possible and will avoid the sort of monolithic scheme that cannot be flexible in meeting the constantly changing demands of the labour market.

Nairobi's 'parking boys'

In Kibera, a slum area of Nairobi, there is a school for poor children who have never been to school and are too old to join regular school; for street children; and for school drop-outs. They are primarily the children of very low-income families. Many of them have to be in the streets earning a living while other children go to school. The programme caters for children between 12 and 19 years old.

Njoki Wainaina, who lives in Nairobi, knows some of the children and the organisation which helps them – the Undugu Society of Kenya.

An Undugu community home. The boys keep rabbits and grow fruit and vegetables to earn extra money

'Undugu' is a Swahili word meaning brotherhood or comradeship. The society was started in 1975 by Father Arnold Grol to help street children. The 'parking boys', as they are popularly known, are named after one of their favourite occupations, helping motorists find parking spaces, for a fee.

Father Grol felt compassion for these boys. For many of them, the streets were their only home, and people had learned to regard them with fear and suspicion, knowing they would not hesitate to grab purses, pick-pocket or steal from cars. His first efforts were to organise them to earn an honest living. Together they started a band and eventually performed for various audiences to earn money.

Over the years Undugu has gained more insight into the problem of destitute children. Today, it focuses on solving problems at source, and on seeking long-term solutions. From rehabilitating street children, the programme has spread to the slum areas from which most of the children come. Special emphasis is placed on keeping the children within the family and the community as far as possible.

Undugu offers a basic three-year programme covering the following subjects: Kiswahili, English, mathematics, business education, social studies, science, agriculture, religious education, music, arts and crafts, home science and physical education. At the end of the three years, the student is expected to have acquired some practical skills as well as a knowledge of literacy, numeracy and business.

Gladys Wambui, co-ordinator of the education programme, came to Undugu after many years of teaching in regular schools. According to her: 'Street children are business people. They are well informed about survival opportunities and are determined to get by against all the odds. After school, many of them work in the slum areas, selling odds and ends, recycling products and providing services such as carrying water. School promises them a better future, but they have to strive harder for it.'

A fourth year course is also offered, but it is optional. This comprises basic training in sheet metal work, carpentry and tailoring at Undugu's workshop, and prepares young people for further training and employment. At this stage, the trainees can produce items that are marketable, find jobs, or opt for an apprenticeship programme. This lasts one to two years, after which the newly qualified can seek formal employment or start their own business. If they decide to set up a business, they can get a loan from Undugu to help them and, if necessary, upgrade their skills in the workshop.

The education programme has four schools in the Kibera, Ngomongo, Pumwani and Mathare slum areas of Nairobi, with a total enrolment of 400. Over the years, it has trained many children whose chances of going to school and earning a living would otherwise be minimal.

Michael

In the metal workshop

Michael Miruru, now 20 years old, joined Undugu in 1982. He came to Nairobi with his mother, four sisters and a younger brother after their father had deserted them in 1980. Michael is the eldest and has to help his mother to support the other children. Although he had started school before they came to Nairobi, he could not continue as his mother could not afford the fees.

Undugu brought them new hope. Michael is now in the final stage of his two-year apprenticeship in sheet metal work. Out of an allowance of about 600 Kenyan shillings (about £18) per month he already helps his mother, who is a vegetable hawker, to educate his brothers and sisters. He has done so well that Undugu plans to employ him at the workshop.

According to Gladys: 'Undugu meets the basic needs of these slum children to learn quickly and get out. Most of them are proud of earning a living. They respect those who respect them. They also have an instinct about people, and can easily identify friends among the various authorities such as police, development and social workers. They will trust and confide in those who are helpful and understanding, but they can also be crafty and evasive. Like everybody else, they are striving for a better life.'

Starehe and the story of Paul Ereng

The Starehe Boys' Centre in Kenya has been supported by SCF since the early 1960s. It is geared specifically to the needs of orphaned and disadvantaged boys, and holds a presidential trophy as the best secondary school in the republic. Up to 1000 boys attend the school, their costs being met through sponsorship. Under a national scheme administered from Starehe, SCF reaches out to sponsor a further 1150 boys and girls in other schools across Kenya. Year after year, their academic results are well above the national average.

The Director, Geoffrey Griffin, tells the story of one of Starehe's better-known ex-pupils.

The Turkana inhabit a bleak, almost rainless area in north-western Kenya. **Paul Ereng**'s family migrated southwards to the more fertile

THE TIMES AT THE OLYMPICS

Ereng moves up from nowhere

From David Miller

With almost biblical simplicity, Paul Ereng, who as a boy was a cow-herd, came down from the high plains of Kenya to win an Olympic gold medal yesterday. If we are astonished by the improbability of his victory, Ereng himself is still reeling in a haze of disbelief.

He not only beat Cruz, the defending champion, but the legendary Aouita, and for hours afterwards he could hardly comprehend the reality of what he had done. Never having competed in a 800 metres until this year, Ereng is yet another phenomenal Kenyan runner. Mike Koskei, the national middle-distance coach, estimates that Ereng can run 1 min 39 sec, some two seconds below Sebastian Coe's seven-year-old world record. "That's what we are aiming for," Koskei said with a laugh.

Ereng's victory, running through from the back of the field after the final bend, past a host of famous names, is partially a story of sacrifice by Nixon Kiprotich, his

Embracing history: Ereng, the unheralded Kenyan, finishes ahead of the best in the world in 1 min 43.45 sec to win the 800 metres gold medal yesterday

colleague. Under Koskei's direction it was planned that Kiprotich, a front-runner, would create a fierce pace that would destroy Barbosa and Cruz, the two Brazilians

Trans-Nzoia district, where they became squatters, living on another man's land and permitted to grow subsistence food for themselves in exchange for labour. Paul's father died of disease in 1974, leaving his mother to bring up the boy and a younger sister with what help could be given by a paternal uncle, a casual labourer. The committee of the local primary school took pity on the children and allowed them to attend with remission of all payments. In 1980 when Paul reached the final year of primary education and had no hope at all of going further, the school headmaster, the local chief and the parish priest jointly recommended him to Starehe where in January 1981 he was granted a form one place made free by sponsorship.

Paul remained in Starehe for five years, obtaining fair 'O' levels and taking a basic accountancy course. He proved to be a pleasant, well-behaved boy and rose to be a house prefect. He showed talent in sports, and with training and encouragement from Starehe's games master, became captain of athletics and did well at the 200 and 400-metre events in inter-school competitions. On leaving Starehe, he got a job in the Post Office.

In late 1987, Paul's athletic ability gained him a track scholarship to an American university. In January 1988 he began, for the first time, to train for the 800-metre event. The rest is history. Nine months later, Paul Ereng's name flashed around the world when he won the Gold Medal in the Olympic Games. Acknowledging the cheers of the crowds in Seoul, Paul had come a long, long way. One of his first acts on returning to Kenya was to visit Starehe and use his locally donated prize-money to become a sponsor himself.

Sierra Leone

The diamond digger's son

This story is told by Christine Varga, until recently a Peace Corps worker with the Boys' Society of Sierra Leone.

Sahr

Sahr's father was a diamond digger. He was an alcoholic and had trouble keeping steady work. Sahr's mother was a petty trader. She loved and pampered him because he was the youngest in the family. Until he was ten, Sahr lived with his parents in Kono, an area of Sierra Leone about 200 miles north-east of the capital, Freetown. Then his parents separated and his mother was unable to support him. He was sent to Freetown to live with an older sister and her husband. The situation in town proved to be equally unstable. After several months of quarrelling, his sister and her husband parted. She fled to Guinea, leaving Sahr with a man who made it very clear that he wanted no responsibility for him. Shortly after his sister left, Sahr found himself on the street.

At first he supported himself though odd jobs, petty thievery and a substantial amount of gambling (bingo and lottery), to which he became addicted. But he soon became incorporated into a sort of minor Mafia common on the streets of large urban centres like Freetown. The patron is usually a man, often himself a former street boy, who makes a living by organising several young rootless boys into a gang. Under the aegis of the patron, or 'bra' as they are called in the local krio, the boys get involved in everything from dealing drugs on the streets and carrying out group burglaries to serving as go-between in prostitution rings. In exchange for their work, the bra 'keeps' them, giving them food, pocket money and a place to sleep.

If the bra is apprehended in any of his illegal exploits, the boys are either themselves caught or they lose their means of support. It was the latter that ended Sahr's two years under an influential bra in the East End of Freetown. Once again, he was alone on the streets.

Not long after Sahr was back on his own, he met Alpha. Alpha was a social worker for the Boys' Society of Sierra Leone, a rehabilitation programme geared toward street boys around greater Freetown. A man in his early twenties, Alpha was himself a former street boy and one of the success stories in the programme. He now held the unique position of social outreach worker for the programme which had brought him in off the streets.

The friendship between Sahr and Alpha grew slowly. Sahr was understandably hesitant to trust adults – especially men – given his background. Alpha would meet him on the street and offer him some food or a bit of spending money. He began telling Sahr of his own experiences on the streets and about his work. Gradually Sahr became an active member of his zone while still living on the street.

As a result of Sahr's enthusiasm, Alpha recommended him for a place in the programme's carpentry training centre. At first, Sahr was reluctant, but in the end he accepted. He had just turned 14, had never been to school, and had no prospects for the future.

In the meantime, Alpha had done some probing and discovered that both Sahr's father and another older sister were living in Freetown. Neither had had any knowledge of Sahr's whereabouts. When Alpha approached Sahr's father, he flatly refused any responsibility for his son. Sahr's sister, though, was anxious to see him and have him to stay. So Sahr went to live with her and attended the training centre.

But Sahr's story does not end so easily. There are still problems. Sahr's sister is 27 years old, a single parent with five small children and no steady employment. The gambling habit Sahr picked up on the streets is still with him. One of his foremost problems is that he spends all his trainee stipend on gambling. At times his work attendance is poor because of his unstable home life and because of his gambling habit. But his supervisors all agree that after a year and a half at the training centre and over two years with the Boys' Society, he has changed markedly.

✗ Disabled children should not be excluded from the opportunities offered to more healthy children. But their needs are often expensive to cater for – especially the cost of specially-trained teachers. The story of Sydwell Nhlabatsi in Swaziland shows how much can be achieved with special facilities. It is notable, however, that Sydwell's success took place in a country with higher school enrolment at all levels, and a higher national income per head than the average for sub-Saharan Africa. The needs of ordinary people are so overwhelming and so difficult to meet, that poor countries often cannot afford the luxury of meeting special needs.

Zimbabwe – special school for the blind

Swaziland

Overcoming disability

Susie Miles, SCF Disability Coordinator in Southern Africa, recounts Sydwell's story.

Sydwell

Sydwell doesn't remember a time when he could hear. It is assumed that he became deaf after he had learned to speak following a serious illness, possibly meningitis. He had to cope with the psychological shock of becoming deaf overnight all alone.

Sydwell was only referred to a special school for the deaf at the age of 13. Before that he suffered the severe handicapping effects of several years of attending his local school with an undetected hearing loss. Usually only profoundly deaf children up to the age of eight are admitted to the school, but he was taken in as a special case

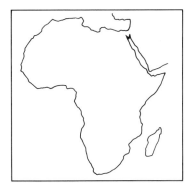

since there was no other special help available for hearing-impaired children at that time.

There was no specialist in the country who could test his hearing and explain that because the damage was permanent, he would have to learn new ways of communicating and, even more important, his family, friends and teachers would have to learn them. Instead, people were impatient with him, not understanding why he didn't always listen, or sometimes simply disobeyed. They didn't realise that his severe hearing loss meant that he could only guess at the words they were saying. His near perfect speech deceived them. They didn't notice that he was speaking slowly and more softly than usual. Nor did they notice that he was beginning to spend more time alone and was becoming shy of people.

In Swaziland it is disrespectful for a child to look at the face of an adult. Now that Sydwell was severely hearing-impaired he relied more and more on visual clues to make sense of what people were saying. However, he was frequently reprimanded for staring too hard into a teacher's face in his efforts to lip-read her words. He was seated so far back in the classroom that learning became more and more difficult. He failed many years of school. Sometimes he was asked to repeat classes and other times he had to be moved up automatically. Every day he was faced with fear and failure.

One of the stories which Sydwell recounts of those days is of being instructed to close his eyes for school prayers. When he plucked up courage to open them again he was all alone. He hadn't been able to 'see' the instruction to open his eyes again!

The many beatings, which resulted from severe learning problems and continual misunderstandings in the classroom led his father to remove him from school and look elsewhere for help. It was then that they heard about Siteki School for the Deaf.

It was clearly a relief for Sydwell to be in the company of other hearing-impaired children. He quickly learned to use informal signs, since the other children were unable to speak. Fortunately there was another boy in his class who had also become deaf a few years before, so they were able to speak to each other in Siswati, the language of Swaziland, which was not taught in the school. The medium of education was English as in the regular schools.

For the first time in his school career, Sydwell was able to understand his teacher, because he was in a class of only eight children. The school had no hearing aids, but the children were encouraged to lip-read and the teaching was less formal than in the regular school.

It took several months for him to relax and enjoy learning since for so many years he had associated learning with fear. He slowly gained confidence, both in and outside the classroom. He began playing football for a local team and made many friends in the small town where the residential school for the deaf was situated. He and a number of other deaf teenagers joined a youth organisation which ran work camps in the school holidays. This could mean staying in a rural area for two weeks to help a community build their own clinic or protection for their water supply. Sydwell mixed well with the other work campers and was elected to take part in an exchange visit to Lesotho.

Sydwell had never passed an exam. If he had remained in his local school, he would never have done so. For the first time since the special school had started, it was decided to enter a number of the oldest pupils for the Standard 5 exam. This is taken in the final year of primary school and qualifies a child to enter secondary education.

Sydwell passed the exam. Instead of following his classmates to the vocational rehabilitation centre in the capital, a special effort was made to obtain a place for Sydwell at an industrial training centre in Manzini, to do a two-year printing course. He stayed with relatives in the town, which is only an hour's journey from his parents' home.

One of ten trainees, Sydwell was the only deaf person in the whole training centre. His instructor was specially briefed on how to communicate most effectively with him. He was fitted with a hearing aid for the first time in his life, which helped a little, but it was difficult for him to adjust to, since he had by now developed his own ways of coping with his impediment.

His instructor was extremely pleased with his progress. Sydwell passed his trade test in January 1989 and has since been employed with a printing firm in Mbabane, 40 kms from Manzini, the capital.

In 1986 a speech and hearing clinic service was set up in all the main hospitals in Swaziland. This service aims to identify speech- and hearing-impaired children as early as possible and to provide appropriate rehabilitation in their home areas. There is a strong focus on schools, so that children like Sydwell can be helped before it is too late.

Unfortunately for Sydwell, this initiative came too late for him to be helped in his local school. In the secure environment of a school for the deaf, however, he soon realised his abilities and regained confidence in himself. He is still shy, especially when meeting new people who don't realise that he is severely disabled. He has, however, made a smooth transition into an independent adult life. He still values the company of his school friends, but is not dependent on them. He has earned the respect of his family through achieving a level of education never thought possible, and by becoming – to their surprise – a major contributor to the family income.

The special needs debate is especially relevant in countries like Sudan and Mozambique where the tragic consequences of civil war are affecting children. Here, many children are so badly injured or traumatised that their minds are effectively frozen. They cannot relate to others and find it impossible to learn when placed in ordinary schools.

In the 1970s, Mozambique's success in achieving universal primary enrolment was quite remarkable. Now many school buildings are completely destroyed and many teachers have been killed or frightened away. In some areas as fast as the debris is reassembled to provide a shelter for teaching, it is torn down again by marauding bandits and rebels. The learning process cannot start for many children until they have been rehabilitated into substitute families or settled into orphanages.

M ozambique *Schools in conflict*

Carolyn Miller, SCF's Field Director in Maputo, shows how schools have become primary targets during the war in Mozambique.

Mozambique – escolinha

Under Portuguese colonial rule many Mozambican children had little or no access to education. One of the most important achievements of independent Mozambique was that, in the five years after 1975, the number of primary and secondary school pupils doubled and there was an even more remarkable four-fold increase in the intermediate fifth and sixth classes. Notable gains were also made in adult literacy.

However, as a result of the war of destabilisation by the MNR there has been a drastic reduction in school attendance, estimated at around 25 per cent. Since the early 1980s, over 2600 primary schools (45 per cent of the total) have been destroyed, affecting about 500,000 pupils and 7000 teachers. Secondary schools, boarding and special schools and teacher training centres have also been robbed of all their equipment; roofs, windows and doors have been taken, burnt or smashed.

Teachers are deliberate targets for attack because of their key role in improving life and conditions in a community. They are often killed or mutilated if captured. The majority of those that escape are displaced within the country, but others are found in refugee camps in neighbouring states.

Within Mozambique SCF mainly works in the province of Zambezia, the most densely populated and one of the worst affected. Seventy-four per cent of the primary schools are closed and 725,000 people have been displaced from their homes and mainly live in accommodation centres. A further 363,000 are affected by severe food shortages. Our health and social workers regularly visit the more secure areas by plane (overland travel is not possible due to rebel attacks) and SCF is carrying out reconstruction and rehabilitation work in several districts.

The district of Morrumbala, for example, was liberated in March 1987. Immediately people started returning from the bush to the relative safety of the district centre. There they were able to build houses and were given food, clothing, a plot of land, seeds and tools. Children who may have been forced to work or fight for the bandits, or who may have witnessed attacks or the death or torture of relations, have been given special assistance.

One of the first priorities has been to provide schooling for the children. Some of the teachers in Morrumbala returned from the provincial capital or other safe places. Classes were initially held, with no materials, under a tree, but gradually conditions have improved. SCF has provided construction materials to schools where only the walls remained intact. While waiting for the arrival of these materials the community built some cane and earth brick structures. Unfortunately, a cyclone destroyed them soon afterwards but they are again being rebuilt.

South Africa

Simon Mkhonza

Jenny Matthews photographed and interviewed 18-year-old Simon Mkhonza in March 1989.

Equal opportunity

'The main problem we're experiencing is the way we're growing up, the way we are taught to grow up. It's tough for children – they don't have many facilities, particularly in education. Education for us blacks is very very poor, you'll find that children only go to school for a few hours. We don't have productive games to give us an insight into things. We grow up in a situation where we rarely have creches so we don't learn games that will help us to develop.

'The education system is also very poor in the sense that it is divided into two. We get what is called "Bantu education" which has less chance of leading to jobs. The white races have what is called "white education" where for example their libraries are well stocked and they have a lot of equipment for science experiments. In our black schools we only have rather poor books for reading and not much else.

'Unfortunately in my country we have the so-called Group Areas Act which was issued long ago and this creates all sorts of problems between the white nation and the black nation. It also creates problems among the blacks because it encourages tribalism and the idea of self-pride for different nations, in such a way that urban dwellers, for example, regard rural dwellers as nothing, the lowest of the low. Those people in the homelands have the poorest soil which isn't at all productive. They have little chance to get jobs. Meanwhile people in the cities get the best. But we're one country and we should have equal opportunities.

'The Group Areas Act puts tribes in different areas and then they say for example, you as a Zulu are superior to the Ndebele, you as Ndebele are the strongest nation, no nation will defeat you, and then they take the Swazis and say you Swazis are the most peace-loving nation so you mustn't let any Sotho come into your country, and in this way this Act created this foolish pride of thinking one nation as the best and the others as inferior. This affects us a lot today and I believe it will in the future.

'Many of us young people feel this constitution and all the institutions must be changed. In fact the majority of people in the country really feel that all such problems must be overcome – reforms must happen. The State still needs security but things like the apartheid system, the Group Areas Act, the division in education – as a majority we really feel there must be some reform in such matters.'

AFRICA'S
DEVELOPMENT
CHALLENGE

*A*frica's development challenge

Prospects for Africa saw Africa as a continent in crisis; two years on, the crisis has yet to pass, and in some countries it is deepening. Overall, incomes have declined at an average rate of 2.5 per cent per annum since 1980, while in some countries child deaths are rising and a smaller proportion of children are going to school.

All countries are finding recovery in the 1980s difficult, but not all have suffered to the same extent. In some countries growth was relatively good in 1988 – over 6 per cent in Kenya and Mali. But with an average annual population growth rate in the region of 3.3 per cent, real economic improvement must not only make up for ground lost in the 1980s, but also compensate for population increases. In Kenya, which has the highest population growth rate in the region at 4.1 per cent per annum, incomes have stood still in the 1980s; good growth was not enough to raise them by more than 1.3 per cent in 1988.

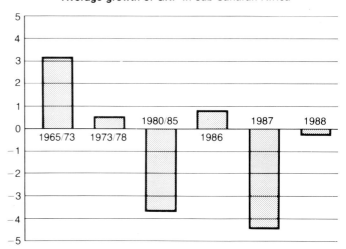

Average growth of GNP in sub-Saharan Africa

Source: World Development, Report 1989, *World Bank, 1988*

The reality for families is illustrated in the stories in this chapter: in the first of the three Kenyan families, Muthoni has not had the advantage of an education which might have helped her make the choice to have fewer children and get a job. She finds it difficult to keep her children healthy and pays nearly a fifth of her monthly income on school fees. For the present, the cycle of poverty is likely to continue for families in her neighbourhood of Kibagare, unless they have special help. There is a marked contrast with Rebecca's family, and still more with Margaret's, both of which have benefited from educated parents lucky enough to have jobs. These contrasts, to a greater or lesser extent, are repeated all over Africa.

Throughout the world people look forward to a better life for themselves and their children, but the present reality for many in

Africa is gloomy. The under five mortality rate (U5MR – the number of deaths per thousand live births) is nearly 300 in Mali and Mozambique: in other words, over a quarter of all the children born there each year do not have a fifth birthday. The child death rate has hardly improved since 1985 in Kenya, Tanzania and Mali, after a deterioration in the first half of the decade. On the other hand, there were relatively fewer infant and child deaths in Nigeria, Senegal and Ghana in 1980–85, although improvements in these countries now appear to have halted.

Primary school enrolment also declined in most sub-Saharan countries in the 1980s although some, such as Nigeria, Senegal and Ghana, diverted scarce resources into maintaining and even improving secondary enrolment. The most marked deterioration was in Tanzania, which had achieved almost 100 per cent primary enrolment by 1980, only to have this slip to about 70 per cent by the middle of the decade.

The story is not one of universal misery and deprivation. Africa is a continent of great contrasts and rich diversity, and some countries have achieved impressive successes. Some, such as Botswana, have maintained their high levels of economic growth and are able to spend enough to educate all their children. Others, such as Senegal, have achieved their target of universal immunisation so almost all Senegalese children are now protected from measles, diphtheria, tetanus, whooping cough and polio.

Kenya

The story of three families

The stories that are told in the course of this chapter have been contributed by Mike Wooldridge, one of the BBC's Africa correspondents, who until 1989 was based in Nairobi.

Muthoni's family

. . . Less than a mile from where I and my family lived in Nairobi is a slum area called Kibagare. More than 2000 people live in shacks that cling somewhat precariously to one side of a valley.

In one of these lives a women called Muthoni. She was born there – she's a second generation slum dweller. Her day begins and ends early. She can hardly afford any paraffin to light a lamp for the evening. Most nights there's nothing for her and her six children to do but go to bed. Her home burnt down last year. She rebuilt it from charred bits of tin, corrugated iron and wood and put a cheerful red 'welcome' sign outside.

There's just a single room, with a dirty sheet strung across the middle to divide the living and sleeping areas. Two beds, a small table and a bench are all the furniture she possesses. She can't afford charcoal, so she sends her oldest children out to collect sticks and cooks over three stones which support her cooking pot. There are no sheets on the beds – she has a couple of blankets to keep off the chill, which can be sharp at this 5500 foot altitude.

Muthoni earns the equivalent of £16.50 a month working at a welfare centre. She spends half of it on maize meal and a few other minor food items; rent uses up another £3, school fees almost the same. There's precious little left over even to buy a bar of soap.

Last year her three-year-old son tipped boiling water on to his head and neck. The hospital told her to buy vaseline, gauze and antibiotics. Muthoni was forced to beg for the money from neighbours and friends, and had to leave the rest of the family while she walked five miles each way with the child to the hospital for each appointment.

Muthoni's neighbours earn their money from prostitution, starting as young as 14; from illegal brewing and selling of a liquor called chang'a, or from reselling charcoal.

Muthoni would like to see at least two children into secondary school because she doesn't want the whole family to be condemned to slum life. Already her oldest child, aged 13, has fallen foul of local thugs and has turned to petty crime. Recently, Muthoni borrowed £8 and got herself sterilised, which she says has brought her some peace of mind. She dreams of having some land of her own one day on which she could build a better home for herself and the children and have a plot alongside it to grow vegetables.

There are thousands of Muthonis in Nairobi and in most big African cities – millions of families with similar pressures on them and similar aspirations. . . .

■ Every child has the right to a standard of living adequate for his or her physical, mental, spiritual, moral and social development. Parents or guardians have the primary responsibility to secure this standard, while the State must provide assistance in case of need.
From the UN Convention on the Rights of the Chi

The prospect of most African countries improving their growth rates is poor in the short term, and most medium-term forecas are not optimistic. Current investment levels are extremely low and foreign private investment is difficult to attract even when the returns are attractive. Wealth is not being generated sufficiently to pay off debts, to save and invest, and to spend on welfare services. Better support from the international community is vital in the for increased aid, new finance and debt relief.

Why do poverty and deprivation in Africa persist, when the maj international finance institutions, such as the World Bank, have promised special treatment for the poorest African countries; whe the British government among others has increased its aid to Afric when the international donor community seems to be making special efforts to address the problems of debt and low economic growth in the least developed countries?

To answer these questions we must look more closely at trade, a and debt.

Africa depends on export earnings to pay for imports and to service its debts. World trade expanded by over 9 per cent in 1988 and in the developing countries as a whole (including those in Sou

America, the Far East and Asia) exports improved by 13 per cent. Overall African exports improved slightly, but contracted by 0.5 per cent in the poorer sub-Saharan region. Most African countries rely on exporting unprocessed or partly processed commodities such as seeds for vegetable oil, tea and coffee, and other tropical products.

Although prices for primary products rose on average in 1988, they had been declining for several previous years. World prices for coffee fell by one-third between March and July 1989, so that earnings from coffee were 30 per cent lower than in 1987 – when they were the lowest they had been for 40 years.

Around 90 per cent of Africa's export earnings will continue to depend on the prices of primary commodities and future prospects are not encouraging. Bad weather and pests such as locusts mean poor harvests for many; recent harvests were good, where the weather was exceptionally favourable.

Even if African countries are able to raise their output and expand their exports – and they are making tremendous efforts to do so – the protectionist policies of the countries with which they trade (the US and the EEC, for example) do not always allow them to compete fairly on the international market. The rich agricultural countries subsidise their own farmers and impose import quotas which often restrict the poorer countries' trading opportunities.

Despite these difficulties, new ideas are being put into practice. Some countries have been able to branch out into new areas of production and export. Zimbabwe, Ethiopia and more recently Kenya, Mauritius and the Ivory Coast now supply growing quantities of cut summer flowers to the European Community. Kenya supplies the EC with three-quarters of its French green bean imports in the summer. Mauritius, the Ivory Coast, Ethiopia and Zimbabwe are now exporting significant amounts of clothing and leather goods.

Outside finance for Africa from the industrialised OECD countries improved in 1988. Although official development assistance (oda) to all developing countries in 1988 was roughly the same in real terms as it was the previous year, total resources for sub-Saharan Africa increased by $1.5 billion in 1988. These increases, however, were mostly due to the timing of payments, and did not necessarily herald an improving longer-term trend.

Despite the increase in the volume of aid, aid per capita is lower now than it was at the beginning of the decade because of population increases.

British aid to sub-Saharan Africa fluctuated during the 1980s. Gross bilateral aid fell from about £357 million in 1980 to £250 million in 1984 in real terms. An increase to £304 million in 1985 was followed by another fall to £268 million in 1986. 1988 saw British aid levels rise back to pre-1980 levels, to £365 million.

As a share of gross national product (GNP), Britain's aid spending rose from 0.28 per cent in 1987 to 0.32 per cent in 1988, the highest oda/GNP ratio since 1985. But the increase is largely the result of the special timing factors affecting other donors.

otham's family

. . . Jotham and his wife Rebecca live in one of the most densely populated rural areas of western Kenya. Jotham was head of a village polytechnic or technical school, then acquired a better paid job with one of the development agencies in Kenya. Rebecca is an agricultural extension officer, advising farmers what to grow. They started their marriage – after Jotham's father had paid Rebecca's a dowry of 12 cows and the equivalent of £750 – on a two and a half acre compound, along with 31 other members of Jotham's family.

Jotham and Rebecca's house might be thought to be a 'mud hut', but he explained to me how complicated it is to build such a house. From the erecting of poles to mark the corners, walls and roof, to the applying of the final coat of mud plaster, takes three weeks. Having built his own house Jotham – as a successful wage earner – had another duty to fulfil before he thought of moving away from the crowded family compound on to land of his own. This was to build a better house for his ageing parents, which he did at a cost of £350 – a square, mud-walled structure with a tin roof.

Then he managed to rent some land; Rebecca put hybrid maize on it and it did very well. They saved hard, and eventually they purchased three acres of land and put on it a brick house with a tiled roof, the grandest anyone in Jotham's family had ever owned. They now have four smartly turned out children. They are still saving for a car, the next priority after building the house and providing for the children's education.

Jotham and Rebecca are representative of what we call a rapidly expanding middle class in Kenya, and it's a development echoed in many African countries. Their relative prosperity brings with it a wide range of responsibilities: the more successful a man becomes, the more he finds members of his 'extended family' calling on him for school fees, loans, help in getting a job and so on. But new wealth trickling through Africa's large family groups makes them increasingly strong economic units.

Jotham has noticed interesting changes in social life in his area. There is now, for example, less casual visiting between one compound and another. Tradition has it that any visitor must be given food, and with all the demands on their money nowadays many people can no longer afford to be so hospitable. Men used to get together to drink millet beer but this is now rare, perhaps because of the influence of religious groups that have proliferated in the area. Social life, he says, is now more centred on the individual compound. Urban 'middle class' life in big cities like Nairobi, Harare and Abidjan is fast emulating urban lifestyles in the West. In Nairobi, maisonettes are sprouting up everywhere – just about accessible to Kenya's 'yuppies', the double income families. There is much concern in the features and letters columns of the local press about the small children who are often left all day in the hands of an 'ayah' – sometimes a young female relative summoned or volunteered from the rural branch of the family. . . .

With much attention being paid to the debt problems of Latin America it is often overlooked that, relative to the size of their economies, African countries' debts are even larger. They have, moreover, continued to increase during the 1980s. Most African debt is owed to governments rather than to commercial banks as in the case of Latin America. By 1987 the debts of the poorest African countries amounted to 83 per cent of their GNPs – nearly double the ratio for the Latin American debtors – and over four times the value of their exports. Even though much of this debt has been acquired on special terms, and despite debt write-offs and other relief measures, the cost of servicing these debts in 1987 absorbed nearly one-fifth of total export earnings. A high proportion of African countries are facing great difficulty in servicing their debt. One symptom of this is their frequent requests for debt rescheduling: in 1980–87, 21 low-income African countries went through no less than 88 reschedulings – about 85 per cent of all such re-arrangements; and 31 African countries are now officially classified as 'debt-distressed'.

The international community has put the problem of developing country debt firmly on its agenda. The International Monetary Fund (IMF) set up two special borrowing facilities for the poorest countries so that the money that was paid back in interest would be re-lent with very low interest and for longer periods than usual. But this recycled money is being paid out very slowly, and the IMF continues to receive from developing countries more money in repayments alone, in addition to interest, than it lends.

The World Bank agreed to reduce the interest on their loans to 13 African countries and promised to lend an additional $400 million a year to the poorest African countries with serious debt problems. But the procedures of the contributing countries are so lengthy that payments are about 20 per cent behind schedule.

Some countries such as West Germany, France and Sweden have cancelled previous export credits, while others, including Britain, have cancelled aid loans or accepted local currency payments. Others have extended payment periods, but this has meant increasing the total sum borrowed and higher interest charges. Several other proposals have been put forward for reducing or cancelling interest, or lengthening grace periods, but objections, most notably from the US, have prevented agreement being reached. The limited agreements reached with commercial banks have made little difference to the poorest countries. While the banks have prepared themselves for possible losses by making provision for unpaid debts, they have not actually cancelled any specific debts owed by particular countries.

If there is to be any prospect of economic recovery for the region, it cannot be achieved through trading surpluses. At present the region is so dependent on the export of raw materials, which continue to sell at very low prices, that surpluses could only be created by cutting imports even further. But this would have a devastating effect on future growth.

Further assistance is therefore needed by Africa in order to improve its savings and investment, to get out of its import dependency to cushion some of the harsher effects of economic reform, and to enable politicians to take effective decisions about expenditure.

Many outside lenders to Africa, including the World Bank, the IMF and donor countries such as Britain, have been reluctant to re-schedule or write off debts, or to increase aid and lending, without some demonstration from African governments that they are taking positive steps to place their economies on a sounder footing. African governments are expected to make spending cuts and to reform and restructure their economies. This process, known as 'structural adjustment', is aimed in the short term at cutting budget deficits, improving efficiency, particularly in agriculture, and promoting exports.

Attempts by African governments to cut their budget deficits have required cutbacks in imports and government spending. These have reduced employment in the public sector, and slashed public works programmes and welfare services. Unemployment has risen, affecting particularly the urban poor who are often unskilled and cannot find alternative jobs easily. In Ghana, tens of thousands of people employed mostly by the Cocoa Marketing Board were made redundant over several years, and most have not yet found other employment.

Wages have fallen, reducing the incomes of the poor even further below the poverty line. Following wage cuts, the average salary of a Ghanaian civil servant meets only 10 per cent of the family's nutritional needs. Reductions in welfare services affect urban and rural poor alike; new services cannot be implemented and the quality of existing services declines.

To stimulate agricultural output, higher prices are being paid to farmers, while government food subsidies are removed. This benefits small farmers who can earn more and reinvest in improved future harvests. But price increases hit the urban poor, so that children's diets shift from protein and fats such as fish, meat, milk, eggs and beans to cheaper foods such as maize with a lower nutritional value. The reduction of food subsidies in Africa, has had according to the Secretary General of the Commonwealth Sir Shridath Ramphal, a 'catastrophic' effect on household well-being.

The United Nations Trade and Development Conference (UNCTAD) has concluded that one of the most pressing problems arising from the effects of these cut-backs is the growing inequality of income within particular countries. To attempt a redistribution c income in favour of the poor poses very difficult political choices fo a government, because it is seen as a threat to the rich and powerful But where the problems of deepening poverty and rising food prices are not addressed, political instability and threat to national securit are likely to follow. In Zambia, where subsidies on maize meal were removed in 1987, there were serious riots in the mining towns of the Copper Belt.

There is a growing body of opinion, including that of the UN Economic Commission for Africa, that some measures to reduce budget deficits in the short term are in conflict with long-term development and the relief of poverty. Public expenditure cuts often hit the poorest groups hardest, women and children in particular. I unemployment is high, women are pushed into casual labour which is poorly paid and precarious. There is also a transfer of costs from the State to the individual, and women – who are providing more and more of their children's health care and education – are suffering particular hardship. Critics of current economic policies claim that this suffering is unnecessary. They say it is possible to design relatively inexpensive special support programmes (such as public employment programmes, unemployment benefits and better credit facilities) for the poorest groups in countries which are undergoing adjustment. The World Bank and other donors recognise that special measures are necessary, and several aid programmes have now been designed to cushion the poor from welfare and employment cuts.

Margaret's family

... Margaret and Richard live 'comfortably' by Kenyan standards, and they acknowledge this. They are buying, on a mortgage, a three-bedroomed two-storey house in a pleasant and secluded area of Nairobi: several neighbouring houses belong to diplomatic missions. They also own two other houses which they rent out, and Richard has inherited a 300 acre farm just to the north of the city.

They have a boy of seven, **Kariuki** and a girl of four, **Wambui**, both attending private schools. As with most Kenyan families, education comes high on their list of spending priorities, after food and mortgage repayments. They could have sent their son to a government school but were put off by the size of the classes – often upwards of 55 pupils.

Margaret and Richard both work, she as a nurse and he as a doctor, and receive free medical cover. They have a car each. They like taking holidays, sometimes on the Kenyan coast, sometimes in Europe. They recently acquired a video camera. They enjoy going to discos and going out to a restaurant once a month. They like entertaining, though Margaret says the increasing cost of alcohol limits the amount of hospitality they can offer: 'It seems no Kenyan likes to leave a house with something left in the bottle,' she says.

But for all their enjoyment of a Westernised lifestyle, they also maintain certain Kenyan traditions. They have given their children African names, though Margaret, as a Roman Catholic, would have liked the children to have first names of Christian origin. But she accepts without hesitation that a husband is head of the household and that his word is final.

When Margaret's mother comes to Nairobi from western Kenya she will not sleep in the same house as her married daughter, but stays in the servants' quarters instead. 'My family are very surprised by our standard of living,' Margaret says. She comes from what she calls a peasant farming family. Her father has two wives. Margaret's own education stopped at the 'O' level stage so that there would be enough money for the younger siblings to go to school as well.

She and Richard say they are limiting themselves to two children – well below the average family size in Kenya – so that they can be sure of giving them the best possible start in life. They hope this will mean university education and professional work for both children.

Like many Kenyans of their status, Margaret and Richard see their urban life as essentially temporary and their Nairobi residence as a 'house' and not a 'home'. Margaret says she would eventually like to make her home on the farm.

Some governments have been keener than others to encourage the growth of a class of people enjoying the creature comforts and opportunities in life that Margaret and Richard have: some have alienated this group to their cost. Margaret and Richard reflect the

African middle-class interest in stability. 'So long as it is peaceful here,' says Margaret, 'we are quite happy.'

There can, of course, be no turning the clock back. Africa is going through one of its phases of rapid social and economic upheaval, touching on the lives of many of its people. Some come through this with a richer quality of life; many others do not.

But traditional African values are far from lost during this process. There is hospitality; the focus on the person rather than the task; a shunning of materialism – at least on the part of the older generation; a respect for age. It would still, I think, be true in much of Africa that a poor man is not a man without a car, but a man without children or cows. Of course, if Africans had not found a way of living with uncertainty – especially with the unpredictability of the climate and thus of the harvest, and grazing for their animals – then they would not have survived at all.

How enduring is Africa's economic crisis? Some believe that prospects are changing, and that the pendulum is starting an upward swing; others believe that it will take decades before real improvements are seen. It is difficult to find reliable indicators of performance. Most recent data on health, education and population growth are often little more than informed 'guesstimates' based, in the best cases, on sample analysis. It is too early to tell exactly how economic reform programmes are working, and to what extent the poorest are directly affected by them.

But the evidence in this book of what is happening to many of Africa's children is enough to show that effective solutions to the crisis have yet to be applied across the continent.

It is of course vital that economies should grow, for without growth there can be no sustainable development or relief of poverty in any country. But as resources are diverted to boost longer-term agricultural and industrial production, and as cuts are made for the sake of efficiency, interim measures are clearly necessary if the health and education needs of the African people are to be met. 'Growth' is something more than an abstract idea which appears in national development plans. Its purpose must be to improve the well-being of human beings and to safeguard future generations. The stories here show how African people can succeed in giving their children a better future, if they are offered the opportunity.

R ecommendations

Having received this book and SCF's evidence from Africa, the Africa Review Group wishes to make the following recommendations:

The Rights of the Child

■ The rights of Africa's children are being neglected day by day but with the adoption of the new United Nations Convention on the Rights of the Child there now exists an internationally agreed legal framework for action. Governments and voluntary organisations need to make full use of this Convention to work for an improvement in conditions for children.

Conflict

■ Governments and the international community as a whole have responsibility for resolving conflicts, of which children are often among the principal victims.

■ Higher priority must be given by governments and voluntary organisations to the protection of children exposed to conflict, especially abandoned and victimised children.

■ Many non-governmental organisations have an outstanding record in coping with the effects of conflict but they need greater recognition themselves and this must be provided by governments.

■ At the international level non-governmental organisations should be offered more creative opportunities to be involved in the decision-making process to solve international problems relating to children.

Emergencies

■ To ensure the effective distribution of relief the skills of the aid agencies and the generosity of the public must be matched by the investment of governments in basic infrastructure such as roads and ports in countries prone to emergencies.

■ In areas prone to drought, governments and aid agencies must help families to improve their food security and level of nutrition, as a safeguard against any emergency.

Health

■ The successful implementation of sustainable health care requires specific actions to end poverty, coupled with low-cost health technologies such as vaccines and oral rehydration therapy. This means carefully planned and targeted programmes involving local people and local resources, as well as adequate external funding.

■ The control of the HIV virus causing AIDS, which is likely to have an impact on every aspect of life and work in many areas of Africa, should be given the highest priority.

■ There must be greater recognition of the central role of women in the evolution of sustainable health care programmes.

■ Governments must allocate more resources to primary health care programmes and consider using non-governmental channels to improve their effectiveness.

Family

■ Agencies and governments should together seek to strengthen the traditional African family structure which in many areas has been so severely shaken by war, migration and economic recession during the last decade.

■ Child care and other key social services need to be adapted to new conditions and designed to strengthen the existing community and extended family structure.

■ Cumbersome and outdated legislation regarding the care of children needs to be overhauled.

Education

■ Long-term development plans in Africa must recognise that basic literacy skills are an essential step towards economic development, better health and more employment.

■ Primary education, still out of reach for many African children, must remain a high priority for governments.

■ A special emphasis must be placed on the education and literacy of both girls and women at every level, recognising their crucial role in the economy.

■ Investment in education will make a substantial contribution to the national economy. This must coincide with progress in general economic development if expectations of school leavers are to be matched.

■ More support needs to be given to appropriate training which enables people to use their own resources and helps the disadvantaged and the disabled to find a place in society.

Development

■ The short-term economic prospects for Africa remain poor. Increased aid, finance, trade concessions and debt relief are essential if the growth rates of the 1970s are to be repeated and if Africa is to recover ground lost during the last decade.

These conclusions are based on the practical experience of those contributing to this book, who include a large number of the professional staff of Save the Children and other agencies. We gladly pass on these recommendations to the public and to other agencies and governments which are working with children in Africa.

In doing so we stress that we are not simply asking for more funds but for a reallocation of resources towards the areas we have identified, to give children in need the support which we know they are owed by the rest of society.

A **ppendix**

The UN Convention on the Rights of the Child

This is a summary of the articles of the UN Convention on the Rights of the Child, but it can only be a guide. Anyone wishing to follow up these rights should read the complete text, obtainable from the Education Unit, Save the Children.

Preamble. The parties to the Convention, recalling the basic principles of the United Nations; reaffirming that children need special care and attention; convinced that the family, as the fundamental group of society and the natural environment for the growth and well-being of all its members and particularly children, should be given the necessary protection; bearing in mind the need for legal protection; and taking account of the importance of cultural values and of international cooperation, have agreed as follows:

1 A child is every human being below the age of 18 years unless he or she has attained majority earlier.

2 Every child has these rights irrespective of race, colour, sex, language, religion, political opinion, disability or any other status, and must be protected against all forms of discrimination or punishment arising from the status of parents or legal guardians.

3 In all legal and other actions concerning children, the best interests of the child are a primary consideration. The child must receive the necessary protection and care from individuals and from institutions which conform with established standards.

4 The State must undertake all appropriate measures to implement these rights. It must implement economic, social and cultural rights in accordance with its available resources.

5 The rights of parents and others responsible for the child to provide appropriate guidance consistent with the child's evolving capacities must be respected.

6 Every child has the inherent right to life. The State shall ensure to the maximum extent possible the survival and development of the child.

7 The child has the right to a name and nationality. The State must ensure the implementation of this right, in particular where the child would otherwise be stateless.

8 The child has a right to preserve his or her identity, including nationality, name and family relations, and must receive appropriate assistance in re-establishing such identity.

9 The child must not be separated from his or her parents unless separation is shown to be in the best interests of the child, as in cases of abuse or neglect. The child has the right to maintain regular contact with the family, and to information about the whereabouts of other members of the family, unless such information would be detrimental to his or her well-being.

10 Applications by a child or his or her parents to leave or enter a state for the purpose of family reunification must be handled positively and humanely. The child has the right to leave any country, and to enter his or her own country, subject only to certain legal restrictions.

11 The State must take measures to combat the illegal transfer and non-return of children abroad.

12 The child has the right to express his or her own views, and to be heard in any judicial and administrative proceedings.

13 The child has a right to freedom of expression and information subject only to certain legal restrictions.

14 The child has a right to freedom of thought, conscience and religion. The rights and duties of parents or guardians in the exercise of this right must be respected.

15 The child has a right to freedom of association and of peaceful assembly.

16 The child has the right to the protection of the law from arbitrary or unlawful interference, or from unlawful attacks on his or her honour and reputation.

17 The child must have access to information from the mass media and other sources, including those which promote social and moral well-being and physical and mental health.

18 Parents or guardians have primary responsibility for bringing up their children. The State must give them appropriate assistance and ensure the development of facilities and services for the care of children.

19 The child must be protected from all forms of violence, injury, abuse, neglect and exploitation, and benefit from social programmes which provide support, investigation and, as appropriate, judicial involvement.

20 Children without families have a right to special protection and to placement in suitable institutions where there is no appropriate alternative family care.

21 The State which recognises or permits the system of adoption must act in the child's best interests and on the basis of reliable information as to the child's status, and with the consent of those concerned. Inter-country adoption may be considered as an alternative, subject to certain safeguards.

22 Children who are refugees or seeking refugee status have a right to appropriate protection and assistance, and to information necessary for family reunification.

23 The mentally or physically disabled child has the right to a full and decent life and should have access to education, training, health care, rehabilitation, preparation for employment and recreation, where possible free of charge. The State shall promote the exchange of appropriate information about the care and treatment of disabled children.

24 Every child has the right to enjoy the highest attainable standard of health and to facilities for the treatment of illness and rehabilitation of health. The State shall take steps to combat disease and malnutrition within the framework of primary health care, through the application of readily available technology and through the provision of adequate nutritious foods and clean drinking water. The State should also take steps to abolish traditional practices prejudicial to children's health.

25 The child who has been placed in care has the right to a periodic review of all circumstances relevant to this placement.

26 The child has the right to benefit from social security in accordance with national law and taking into account the circumstances of the child.

27 Every child has the right to a standard of living adequate for his or her physical, mental, spiritual, moral and social development. Parents or guardians have the primary responsibility to secure this standard, while the State must provide assistance in case of need.

28 The child has a right to education. The State shall make primary education free and compulsory and shall encourage the development of secondary and higher education, making education accessible to all and encouraging regular attendance at school.

29 The aims of education must include the development of the child's personality and ability, preparation for a responsible life, respect for cultural identity and values, and respect for the natural environment.

30 Children from minority or indigenous communities have the right to enjoy their own culture, religion and language.

31 The child has a right to rest and leisure, to engage in play and recreation, and to participate freely in cultural life and the arts.

32 The child has a right to be protected from economic exploitation and from work likely to be hazardous or harmful to education, health or development. The State shall set minimum ages and conditions of employment.

33 The child has the right to protection from the illegal use of drugs and from traffic in drugs.

34 The child must be protected from all forms of sexual exploitation and abuse, including the use of children for prostitution or pornography.

35 The State must prevent the abduction, sale of or traffic in children for any purpose.

36 The State must protect the child against all other forms of exploitation prejudicial to his or her welfare.

37 No child may be subjected to torture, cruel, inhuman and degrading treatment, or punishment, arbitrary arrest, life imprisonment or capital punishment. The child has a right to be treated with dignity, to be given a fair trial, and to receive legal assistance.

38 No child under 15 should take direct part in armed conflict or be recruited into the armed forces, and priority in recruitment should be given to older children. The State must ensure the protection and care of children affected by armed conflict.

39 A child who has been the victim of any form of neglect, abuse, torture, degrading treatment or armed conflict must be guaranteed full recovery and social reintegration in an appropriate environment.

40 A child accused of breaking the law has a right to be presumed innocent until proved guilty, to receive a fair hearing, to refuse to give evidence and to have the assistance of an interpreter. The State is encouraged to promote laws and procedures which specifically apply to children.

41 These rights do not affect any national or international law which may already have set a higher standard of children's rights.

42 The rights must be made widely known in a form which can be understood by both children and adults.

For further reference, see *The International Law on the Rights of the Child*, Geraldine Van Bueren, OUP, 1990.